ENDonomics
Default, Deflation, Derivatives & the End of the United States as We Know It

Jake Shannon

ENDonomics: Default, Deflation, Derivatives & the End of the United States as We Know It
ISBN-10: 1479203688
ISBN-13: 978-1479203680
Copyright © 2012 by Jake Shannon

"I love the US Republic, and I hate the US Empire."
—Johan Galtung

Thanks

To those who influenced me directly or indirectly through their works: Joseph Fuhrig, Benoit Mandelbrot, Jeffrey Rogers Hummel, Carlos Blanco, Johan Galtung, Peter Boettke, Institute for Humane Studies, Kevin Dowd, Center for Independent Thought, Dierdre McCloskey, Laissez Faire Books, Tyler Cowen, and Nassim Taleb.

Contents

Chapter 1

Introduction

THIS IS AN OPTIMISTIC love-story with a rather pessimistic sounding title. I absolutely love the United States for its role in the history of human liberty and prosperity. Having said that, I believe centralized economic planning will be the end of the United States as we know it. As such, ENDonomics is the study of one of the two possible scenarios:

> 1. The end of the United States Empire and how it was crushed under the weight of its own debt and corrupt monetary and taxation system. In such a scenario, ENDonomics will also include the study of the end of modern financial economics/financial engineering that relies so heavily upon the concept of the risk-free rate of return and "fair value," which have proven to be a myth.
>
> Or
>
> 2. The end of central banking and, in particular, the end of the Federal Reserve and the U.S.'s current system of debt and taxation, thereby ending the United States as we know it while allowing for an American jubilee and economic renaissance.

Though people seem to increasingly understand the way fractional reserve banking and the Federal Reserve System contribute

to inflation,[1] the economy is incredibly complex, and few seem
to understand how rampant debt destruction (that is, private and
public bankruptcies), regulations, and onerous derivative liabilities
lead to a massive deflation and the collapse of our financial system.
My first endeavor in this book is to illustrate that the U.S. is, in
fact, currently in a deflationary environment.

Then comes the question: who benefits from our current monetary and regulatory framework? Public Choice economists have
well shown that it is not only actors in the private economy that are
motivated by self-interest, but also politicians and policy-makers.[2]
This book is also an attempt to throw light on how the "power
elite" in our modern world — central bankers, government regulators, corporate CEOs, their lobbyists, and others that seek power
— actively create the consolidation and concentration of power
into the hands of a few as opposed to fostering independence, responsibility, and liberty for all.

In this book I describe what is currently going on in this economy — why, despite all the "quantitative easing" that has been
on-going, the U.S. is still in deflation. It explains the current debt-
deflation and the implications in this modern world of defaults and
derivatives. If this book advocates anything, it advocates honest,
straightforward language and honest, straightforward money. As
Dr. Thomas Szasz writes:

> Orderly human relations depend on the proper func-
> tioning of speech, speakers and listeners attaching the
> same meaning to words. The languages we speak and
> how well or poorly we speak them define who we are
> and largely determine who the persons near and dear
> to us are. Words have standardized meanings... Safe-
> guarding the fixity of the meaning of words (and other

---

[1]As used in this book, inflation means an increase in money supply and deflation a drop in the level of the money supply and not changes in the "general"
price level, unless otherwise indicated.

[2]http://www.econlib.org/library/Enc/PublicChoice.html

symbols) is essential for the integrity and pursuit of the sciences and is indispensable for law, economics, commerce, and honest dealing among upright persons. Conversely, corrupting the meaning of words undermines their integrity, obstructs cultural and scientific progress, and hinders honest discourse among people.

Anchoring money in an objective standard (gold) serves the interests of free trade, the security of property, and personal liberty. Anchoring diagnosis in an objective standard (somatic pathology) serves the interests of medical science, sound medical practice, and personal liberty. Dislodging the meaning of these symbols from their precisely defined positions — legitimizing fiat money and fiat diagnosis as 'real' money and real diagnosis — serves the interests of the new political class, the pharmacrats.

As long as the gold standard was the accepted measure of money, no abstract monetary standard, or 'numeraire,' was needed; similarly, as long as the gold standard of disease was the accepted measure of disease, no abstract disease standard, or 'diagnostic numeraire,' was needed. (Szasz 2001, 53)

Fiat money expands and contracts creating both inflation and deflation, distorting the information conveyed via the price system. I focus here on the "contraction" portion of the 'business cycle' — that cycle of booms and busts caused by the monetary policy of the Federal Reserve Bank. My perspective is a hybrid one, a composite of the Public Choice and Austrian schools of economics, as well as that of a financial "quant."[3] Austrian economics, modern Financial

---

[3]If you are not familiar with what a financial "quant" does, you can read up more here: http://en.wikipedia.org/wiki/Master_of_Quantitative_Finance

Economics,[4] and the fractal finance of Benoit Mandelbrot have almost equally seduced me, and so has my experience as a former 'Manager of Technical Oversight for Complex Instruments while with the Analytics and Valuation team at Indymac Bank, the first bank to get nationalized during this financial crisis.[5] I also seek to reconcile proto-Monetarist Irving Fischer's complementary concept of debt-deflation, in simple straightforward language, with the powerful explanatory model of the Austrian Business Cycle Theory (ABCT). Tyler Cowen's book *Risk and Business Cycles* (1998) has played a major role in achieving a better, integrated understanding of risk-based modern financial economics with regards to the ABCT. In particular, I seek to explain the "credit crunch" portion of the ABCT theory and to look into the incentives and the prospects for deflation, default, and derivative liabilities with regards to the global economy and the coming end of the United States as we know it.

Wikipedia, the website inspired by Nobel prize winning Austrian economist F.A. Hayek,[6] summarizes the ABCT this way:

> Low interest rates tend to stimulate borrowing from the banking system. This expansion of credit causes an expansion of the supply of money, through the money creation process in a fractional reserve banking system. It is asserted that this leads to an unsustainable credit-sourced boom during which the artificially stimulated borrowing seeks out diminishing investment opportunities. Proponents hold that a credit-sourced boom results in widespread malinvestments.

---

[4]You can find more on Financial Economics on http://en.wikipedia.org/wiki/Financial_economics

[5]I was "Manager of Technical Oversight for Complex Instruments" at Indymac Bank between 2004 and 2006, and as one of my colleagues so kindly noted on my LinkedIn.com page (http://www.linkedin.com/in/jakeshannon): "At Indymac, Jake showed great foresight about upcoming market trends and was prescient and vocal about the risks forming in the housing market."

[6]http://online.wsj.com/article/SB123976347774119699.html

Introduction

In the theory, a correction or "credit crunch" – commonly called a "recession" or "bust" – occurs when exponential credit creation cannot be sustained. Then the money supply suddenly and sharply contracts when markets finally "clear", causing resources to be reallocated back towards more efficient uses (emphasis mine).[7]

For long, I've refrained from writing a book on finance and economics because it is a very complex, nuanced, and rapidly evolving subject, but I seem to keep coming back to the themes I present in *ENDonomics* in my conversations on my radio show and on social media. Frankly, I feel the time is ripe for a book expressing and explaining my current thoughts on the subject. It is not an attempt to make the already long list of books[8] explaining the credit crisis of 2007/2008 any longer; it is more an addition to the even longer tradition that seeks to awaken people up to the dangers of central economic planning.

> The present financial crisis has set in bold relief the Jekyll and Hyde nature of contemporary central banks. It has made apparent both our utter dependence on such banks as instruments for assuring the continuous flow of credit in the aftermath of a financial bust and the same institutions' capacity to fuel the financial booms that make severe busts possible in the first place. (Selgin 2010)[9]

The Federal Reserve Bank and the global shadow banking system has not just been a failure;[10] it, along with other forms of central economic planning, will ultimately bring the end of the United

---

[7]http://en.wikipedia.org/wiki/Austrian_business_cycle_theory

[8]A long list is available on http://papers.ssrn.com/sol3/papers.cfm?abstract_id=1949908

[9]You can also view the article on http://www.independent.org/publications/tir/article.asp?a=774.

[10]http://www.cato.org/publications/working-paper/has-fed-been-failure

States as we know it. It is a dream of mine that ENDonomics will eventually become accepted as the economic study of how to end Central Banking.

Chapter 2

Deflation: Decreasing The Supply Of Money And Credit

"Cui bono?"
—Marcus Tillius Cicero, section 84, Pro Roscio
Amerino

GOVERNMENTS ARE FUNDED in two basic ways — via taxation and via borrowing (in addition to a few lesser methods like privatization and seigniorage). To better comprehend the economic system of the United States of America, one must first understand the borrowing relationship between the United States Treasury and the Federal Reserve System and the tax relationship between the Treasury and U.S. citizens. For the United States, the last century has been one of deficits and a growing national debt. In simple terms, a deficit occurs whenever you spend more than you have. So every time the federal government spends more than it has, it must issue a debt instrument or an I.O.U., usually a U.S. Treasury bond, to cover the expense.

As of this writing, the National Debt towers above $15 trillion.[1] The debt per citizen is nearly $50k, but the debt per U.S. taxpayer is approximately $135k. When you include the total amount of unfunded U.S. liabilities in the U.S. — such as Social Security and Medicare — the costs of unfunded liabilities grew to $33.8 trillion in fiscal 2011![2] The U.S. is one of those rare governments that use accrual accounting that counts the cost of promises made,

---

[1] http://www.usdebtclock.org
[2] http://www.gao.gov/financial/fy2011/11frusg.pdf

not just cash paid. Keep in mind that the total value of all the publicly traded companies in the U.S. is only $13.1 trillion, less than half of the U.S. unfunded obligations.[3] Even if you were to add in $6.2 trillion, the total value of all the homes in the U.S.,[4] there would still not be enough to pay these false-promises.

It is truly sobering to ponder the extent of revenue that the IRS must collect to pay the Treasury's bondholders (largely the Federal Reserve and foreign governments with the top five foreign bondholders being China, Japan, United Kingdom, Oil Exporters, and Caribbean Banking Centers).[5] The Federal Reserve banking cartel buys these bonds with paper currency literally created out of thin air on the promise that the government will pay the Federal Reserve back, both the principal and a fixed rate of interest. In our current fiat currency scheme, debt is essentially money. In exchange for this ongoing cash flow in the form of interest payment, the Federal Reserve literally creates money through manipulated ledger accounts and gives it to the Treasury.

How does the Treasury generate revenue to repay its debt to the Federal Reserve? Primarily, it is through taxation (income, payroll, and corporate). The biggest source of tax revenue, your income taxes, goes directly to pay off, in large part, the central banker that loaned it the money. The 16th Amendment essentially made the American people, via the Internal Revenue Service, surety for the debts of the political and monetary decision makers within the United States government.

In an inflation, this money "borrowed" from the Federal Reserve trickles into the economy as the government spends it and finds its way into private banks. Once there, the inflation amplifies through the magic of what is known as "fractional-reserve" banking. In a nutshell, "fractional reserve" banking means that banks must, by law, maintain only a fraction of the actual reserves on-hand (while their ledgers falsely say they have the whole amount);

[3]http://web.wilshire.com/Indexes/Broad/Wilshire5000/
[4]http://www.freddiemac.com/investors/pdffiles/investor-presentation.pdf
[5]http://www.treas.gov/tic/mfh.txt

the currency is inflated and the risk of bank runs remains perennial. This inflationary process is documented in the Federal Reserves' own manual *Modern Money Mechanics*, originally published by the Federal Reserve Bank of Chicago:

> Carried through to theoretical limits, the initial $10,000 of reserves distributed within the banking system gives rise to an expansion of $90,000 in bank credit (loans and investments) and supports a total of $100,000 in new deposits under a 10 percent reserve requirement. (Federal Reserve Bank of Chicago 1971, 8)

In the modern age of TARP and Federal bailouts, many people fear inflation (or even worse, hyper-inflation), and that is completely understandable since inflation is ultimately a form of "secret" taxation, where those who spend the fiat currency nearest to its inception have stronger purchasing power at the expense of those who'll have the money eventually "trickle down" to them. However, none of the stimulus money has "trickled down" to create inflation because it was used by banks to shore up their bad derivative positions, and still, it wasn't enough.

Keep in mind that the size of the derivatives market is unearthly. The Bank for International Settlements (BIS) puts the nominal value of outstanding over-the-counter derivatives in June of 2011 at $707 trillion dollars.[6] Paul Wilmott, a Ph.D. in applied mathematics from Oxford, estimates it at about $1.2 quadrillion (to gain some perspective on how large a number that is — a quadrillion is one thousand trillion. A trillion is one thousand billion. A billion is one thousand million. A million is one thousand thousand). The $1.2 quadrillion derivatives market is approximately 20 times the size of the world economy.[7]

---

[6]http://www.bis.org/statistics/derstats.htm
[7]http://www.dailyfinance.com/2010/06/09/
risk-quadrillion-derivatives-market-gdp/

Banks are hoarding cash in expectation of expected payouts on anywhere from $200bn to $1tn — no one knows the real amount, adding to volatility. If you remember, defaulted credit derivatives were linked to the collapse of Lehman Brothers, the government's seizure of mortgage giants Fannie Mae (FNM) and Freddie Mac (FRE), the government's rescue of American International Group (AIG), and the failure of Washington Mutual (WM).

Debt and bank liabilities are the reason why none of the stimulus money has been "trickling down" and why the credit crunch continues to lurch forward. To pay for the entire recent "non-trickling-down" stimulus programs, the U.S. Treasury and its partner-in-crime, the Federal Reserve Bank, have not been printing money. Instead, the Treasury has been issuing debt, in record amounts, for the past few years and will likely continue to do so until the American economy collapses under the weight of this debt. This type of borrowing is deflationary since people aren't spending newly printed money; instead, investors are loaning it to the Federal government at almost a 0% rate of return! The Fed is sucking money out of the economy via Treasury auctions. This deflation is why institutional investors are buying treasuries like crazy, despite low yields (whether the price fixing in favor of low interest rates is done by a central bank or more surreptitiously, as in the recent LIBOR scandal). In a deflationary environment, you don't need a return on your investment (that is, yields) to make money; you just need a return of your investment (because each dollar becomes worth more during deflation).

What then should we expect the government to do when tax revenues are no longer sufficient to even pay the interest on the debt, let alone pay down the principal? If you think with your 'cui bono' hat on, the mostly likely scenario is one of low interest rates and massive deflation, as that would benefit the bankers most by increasing the value of their assets (since the price of bonds are inversely related to interest rates and since the loans that they've made get repaid in dollars that are worth more in real terms). The case for a 'cui bono' deflation scenario is compelling. The U.S.

10

government is mostly borrowing its way to solvency these days, not printing it via the Federal Reserve. The U.S. Treasury Department auctions are setting records for sales of federal bonds and T-bills.[8] (They are so averse to the printing press that the Treasury is even raiding a federal pension fund known as the G-Fund to cover their expenditures.[9]) These sales records are being set despite the interest paid on these debt instruments being at record lows. This may sound strange until you realize that this insatiable demand for U.S. debt is not driven by the interest paid on them.

In a deflationary scenario, all you have to do is hold the debt to make money; interest isn't needed to make money since as prices fall during a deflation, each dollar buys more than it could earlier. Granted, the Federal Reserve is printing money, but it won't 'trickle down' since the banks are using the stimulus money to shore up their capital reserves due to the trillions of dollars of bad loans they've made and the disastrous credit derivative positions they hold. If the banks were to show the real market value (not mark-to-model values) of their balance sheets, they would be shown to be insolvent.

As shown earlier, when the fiat money created from the Federal Reserve reaches private banks, inflation accelerates as loans to businesses and individuals explode through fractional reserve banking. But when these loans go bad and individuals and businesses default on their obligations to pay back the loan, that money is simply destroyed. Loan defaults are not inflationary, they are deflationary and loan defaults are at an all time high.

The Case-Schiller Index showed deflation in home prices again in 2011, down another 4%.[10] Consumer prices, too (not just big ticket items, like housing), show that we are in a deflation. According to a new report by the Commerce Department, even consumer

---

[8]http://www.bloomberg.com/apps/news?pid=newsarchive&sid=aEZxetP0Q2Zw

[9]http://www.reuters.com/article/2012/01/17/us-usa-debt-treasury-idUSTRE80G20R20120117

[10]http://www.standardandpoors.com/indices/sp-case-shiller-home-price-indices/en/us/?indexId=spusa-cashpidff--p-us----

prices fell during the month of June, 2011. What's more, private salary and wage income *fell* in June, 2011.[11] Wages are deflating in real terms:

> ...median wages for men between 30 and 50 dropped 27 percent — to $33,000 a year from 1969 to 2009, according to an analysis by Michael Greenstone, a Massachusetts Institute of Technology economics professor who was chief economist for Obama's Council of Economic Advisers.[12]

Even the Quantity Theory of Money[13] seems to point to a sharp deflationary scenario since the velocity of money is low and dropping. This means despite the money being pumped into the economy, people are still clinging to their dollars. As Figure 1 shows, M2 velocity is now at the lowest it has been since the 1950s.

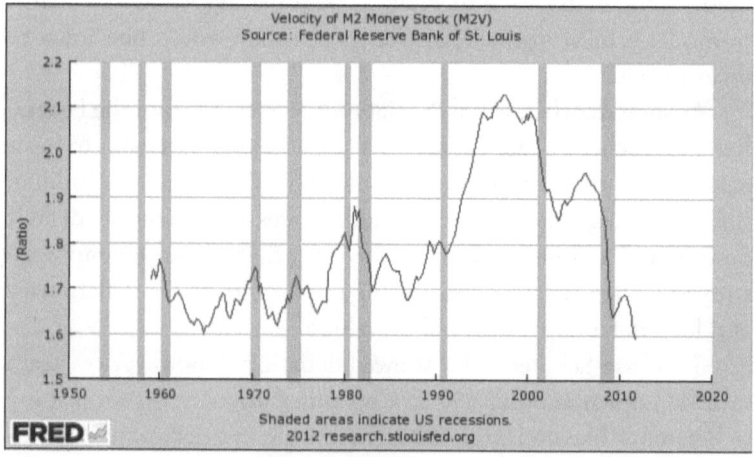

Figure 1

---

[11]http://bea.gov/newsreleases/national/pi/pinewsrelease.htm

[12]http://www.bloomberg.com/news/print/2011-08-25/ obama-seeks-jobs-plan-as-u-s-workingman-status-further-erodes.html

[13]http://en.wikipedia.org/wiki/Quantity_theory_of_money

Deflation

Price Deflation is not Monetary Deflation

Now, I want it to be clear that when I talk about deflation, I am talking about a drop in the level of the supply of money and credit, and when I talk about inflation, I am talking about an increase in the supply of money and credit; I am not talking about the "general" price level. Some prices can rise in a deflationary scenario, due to demand increases or supply restrictions or regulatory influences.

Often effects of changes in political economy can appear as effects from the change of money supply (that is, inflation). For example, despite what your favorite gold-sponsored talk radio show host might have you believe, the recent price of gold has been driven more by the increased global demand for gold due the decriminalization of private ownership in China rather than by inflationary pressures. In October 2002, China authorized private ownership of gold for the first time in 50 years. Demand just increased by a potential 1.3 billion since then. Do you note the interesting correlation between this recent spike in demand and the price of gold?

Let's just assume only 1% of all Chinese citizens jumped on the gold bandwagon; that would still be *thirteen million* buyers. If each of them purchased just 4 ounces of gold, that would still be 1474 metric tons — more than half of all the gold mined in 2001. According to the World Gold Council, 2,604 metric tons were mined in 2001. That's one percent buying just 4 ounces. Now, you can see the real driver of gold prices over the last decade.

In 2010, the yearly demand for gold in China outpaced the combined total of the United States and European Union for the first time. That happened along with triple-digit increases in demand from France, Germany, and Switzerland. The important fact that cannot be underestimated is that the annual buying of gold grew at a 7.5% compounded annual growth rate in the decade after the Chinese government eliminated the last controls on the gold market, that is, from 2001 to 2010. India, the second most populated country on Earth, is also demanding more and more gold.[14]

For example, many people buying gold today don't realize that during the Great Depression people held onto gold as a hedge not against inflation, but against deflation! During the Depression, prices were falling as they are now. However, back then, the price of gold was fixed by law, and as such, it was a great store of value! Then again, in 1933, America was the world's greatest creditor; today, America is the world's greatest debtor. The world is upside down, largely because we've all accepted the upside-down notion that debt equals money.

The "Paul Revere"s of Deflation

Evidence of deflation is everywhere, and there have been a number of people warning about it. David Goldman, the global head of debt research for Banc of America Securities and earlier global head of credit strategy at Credit Suisse, writes:

> The great deflationary wind blowing through markets has brought down all asset prices except for those that directly benefit from deflation, namely bonds.[15]

Famed economist Nouriel Roubini has been suggesting people invest in cash[16] because of global deflationary pressures.[17, 18] His associate and author of the best selling *The Black Swan*, Nassim Taleb, said on the Charlie Rose show that Roubini was too bullish

---

[14]http://www.gold.org/investment/research/regular_reports/gold_demand_trends/

[15]http://seekingalpha.com/article/284779
-the-great-hedge-fund-de-levering-event-has-arrived

[16]http://nourielroubini.blogspot.com/2011/08/
nouriel-roubini-invest-in-cash.html

[17]http://nourielroubini.blogspot.com/2010/01/
roubini-there-is-global-deflationary.html

[18]http://www.forbes.com/2008/10/29/stagnation-recession-deflation-oped-cx_nr_1030roubini.html

with regards to his deflationary views and that there was a very real
risk of massive deflation.[19] Taleb's been advising Universa, a Santa
Monica, California-based firm to invest their clients' funds under
the premise that no one can know where inflation is headed.[20]

Forecaster Bob Prechter makes some interesting succinct ob-
servations, too. First, he notes that banks are heavily invested in
mortgages (thanks to purchases of federal agency securities) that
have homes as collateral; these homes are falling more and more
in dollar value (price deflation). Second, he notes that the availability of small business loans have fallen to their lowest rate since
1980, further proving that the "credit crunch" (that is, monetary
deflation) is very real. In addition, banks have severely tightened
their lending standards, restricting the supply of credit even further. Commercial and personal bankruptcy statistics are also at an
all time high fueling debt-deflation.

When I first described the deflation we were experiencing in my
2009 release *Anomaly: Revolutionary Knowledge in Everyday Life*, I
didn't know of any other proponents of Austrian Economics that
were trying to alert people to the deflation. That's why I was particularly thrilled to read Vijay Boyapati's 2010 article titled 'Why
Credit Deflation is More Likely Than Mass Inflation: An Overview
of the Inflation versus Deflation Debate',[21] where he takes the traditional causal relationship of the money multiplier theory of lending to task and explains why bank credit deflation is probable:

> Several Austrians have predicted that the expansion
> of the Fed's balance sheet, and attendant creation of
> new reserves, will result in a significant growth in the
> issuance of credit and, eventually, a commensurately
> large increase in prices. Some have even predicted that

---

[19]http://www.charlierose.com/view/transcript/9713?pagenum=2
[20]http://www.bloomberg.com/apps/news?pid=newsarchive&sid=
aDVgqxiT9RSg
[21]http://www.scribd.com/doc/66631493/Austrian-Econ-Deflation

the massive creation of new reserves will cause hyper-inflation. However, as explained in the section on Federal Reserve policy and credit expansion, commercial banks are not constrained by reserves when making loans. Prior to the housing bust, the creation of reserves followed, rather than preceded, an increase in the aggregate issuance of loans. Thus, the creation of new reserves per se tells us little about whether banks will be willing to issue new loans.

The enormity of the credit expansion that took place during the housing boom and the corresponding scale of the misallocation of capital left trillions of dollars of loans losses sitting on the balance sheets of commercial banks when the bust arrived. The losses, which rendered many banks insolvent and many others capital constrained, severely restricted the willingness of banks to issue loans to the public, both for regulatory and prudential reasons. The reduced rate of loan issuance and reduced public desire to take on more debt, resulted in a decrease in the aggregate amount of credit in the economy. While the Federal Reserve has the theoretical power to force the resumption in credit expansion by monetizing enough public debt that the losses from the housing bust were wiped away, it is unlikely to do so. The Fed was created for the benefit of the banking class and while it remains under the control of that class it will not pursue a policy that would lead to a breakdown in the monetary system from which the banking class profits. However, the Fed is also unlikely to allow an untrammeled deflation to run its full course, given the risk of political unrest that might arise. Therefore, the Federal Reserve's most likely course of action is to keep the mortgage market, in which most of the losses are concentrated, in a sort of stasis, where losses are acknowledged slowly over time. Such a policy, which might well be called "controlled deflation," would lead to a prolonged period of high unemployment and slow growth, as capital was only slowly reallocated to satisfy consumer preferences. Further, the insufficient or barely sufficient creation of new credit to make up for debt paid down, or defaulted on, would cause a low growth in aggregate prices, which might occasionally become negative. Not until the losses of the housing boom are fully cleared — which might takes years under a policy of controlled deflation — should we expect an inflationary credit expansion and a significant rise in prices.[22]

Austrian economics aside, deflation is such a real concern to those "in the trenches" that, despite all the recent talk about the debt ceiling and the risk of the United States defaulting on its debts, investors are still buying bonds:

> One would imagine that, with America skidding into a high impact debt-ceiling / default wall like an 18 wheeler semi with burned up brakes, treasury bonds would fall in value (and yields rise) as horrified holders ran for the hills. The fact that Uncle Sam could lose his vaunted 'AAA' status even if a deal gets done should further underscore the "dump bonds" notion.

> Nope. Bonds have rocketed *higher* instead — registering a big, bold, high volume breakout on the charts. Yields at the long end of the curve, which move inversely to bond prices, have fittingly dropped to nine-month lows.[23]

---

[22]http://www.scribd.com/doc/66631493/Austrian-Econ-Deflation
[23]http://www.businessinsider.com/global-macro-notes-long-bonds-cheering-the-tea-party-and-deflation-2011-8

Well, Uncle Sam did lose its 'AAA' status, at least with Standard & Poor's (Moody's & Fitch still give a 'AAA' to U.S. securities as of this writing). To further prove that the deflation we're in is still here and only getting worse, the Bank of NY Mellon has even started to charge a fee to large custodial customers to hold cash (note that banks usually pay a positive interest rate to hold cash; this is a negative rate to hold their cash)!

> In reaction, Bank of New York, the biggest custodial bank in the U.S., said that it will charge 0.13%, plus an additional fee if the one-month Treasury yield falls below zero on depositors that have accounts with an average monthly balance of $50 million "per client relationship," according to a letter reviewed by The Wall Street Journal.[24]

There has been a huge credit crunch (that is, deflation) since September 2008. Though there has been "quantitative easing" going on, it has simply not been enough. Even the economics blogosphere is buzzing about deflation:

> The Fed is terrified of the U.S. economy falling into a deflationary death-spiral: Lack of liquidity, leading to lower prices, leading to unemployment, leading to lower consumption, leading to still lower prices, the entire economy grinding down to a halt. So the Fed has bought up assets of all kinds, in order to inject liquidity into the system, and buoy asset price levels so as to prevent this deflationary deep-freeze — and will continue to do so. After all, when your only tool is a hammer, every problem looks like a nail.

---

[24]http://blogs.barrons.com/stockstowatchtoday/2011/08/04/
b-of-ny-mellon-charges-to-hold-cash-deflation-ho/

But this Fed policy — call it "money-printing", call it "liquidity injections", call it "asset price stabilization" — has been overwhelmed by the credit contraction. Just as the Federal government has been unable to fill in the fall in aggregate demand by way of stimulus, the Fed has expanded its balance sheet from some $900 billion in the Fall of '08, to about $2.3 trillion today — but that additional $1.4 trillion has been no match for the loss of credit. At best, the Fed has been able to alleviate the worst effects of the deflation — it certainly has not turned the deflationary environment into anything resembling inflation.[25]

And this global deflation shows little sign of abating. It seems likely to take down the Euro[26] and has plagued Japan for decades, despite the efforts of their central banks. The world's three biggest economies (the United States, China, and Japan) are all in real big trouble, and it seems all will collapse sooner rather than later. China is calling its bankruptcy "deferred loan payments" now.[27] Those using derivatives to insure their investments in China's debt are now showing concern over default:

> Five-year credit-default swaps insuring against default on China's sovereign debt rose 3.2 basis points recently to 149.66 basis points, according to data provider CMA.[28]

---

[25]http://www.zerohedge.com/article/guest-post-how-hyperinflation-will-happen

[26]http://www.dailymail.co.uk/news/article-2068138/Britain-joins-multi-billion-pound-global-bailout-key-banks-face-new-credit- crunch.html

[27]http://www.chinadaily.com.cn/bizchina/2011-12/26/content_14326726.htm

[28]http://www.chinadaily.com.cn/bizchina/2011-12/26/content_14326726.htm

Japan's public debt is the largest in the world (if you don't count unfunded liabilities of the U.S., of course), just a smidge under ¥1 quadrillion.[29] Again, those using derivatives to insure their investments in Japan's debt are concerned, too, it seems given the rising costs of credit-default swaps on Japan's public debt.[30] Japan seems to be the crystal ball to gaze into if we want to look at the future of the American economy; it's a country with similar problems with regards to debt, central banking, and age demographics:

> Deflation will steadily sap nominal growth, depriving the government of revenue, until one day Japan will no longer be able to finance its borrowing, Jerram said. The country will either default on a debt of about twice the size of the economy or debase its currency to reduce the real value of liabilities.
>
> ...During a visit shortly afterward to Tokyo, he urged his Japanese counterparts to work with the Finance Ministry to buy more government bonds to keep interest rates low and cut taxes to spur consumer spending.[31]

Even those that seem to have no worries about deflation feel a need to explain away the obvious:

> Fundamentally, 2.0% 10-year Treasury yields (TNX, TLT) can only be explained in terms of expectations of a 1930's U.S. Great Depression-type scenario coupled with deflation. Similarly, such low yields might

---

[29]http://www.google.com/hostednews/afp/article/
ALeqM5jmG-zGeMIIxTJ6kL9M3u9k7V3knw?docId=CNG.
ed2d1c76e347dd9b69977fa6792108fd.6e1

[30]http://www.ft.com/cms/s/0/720ec456-e4ed-11e0-9aa8-00144feabdc0.
html

[31]http://www.bloomberg.com/news/2011-01-13/
japan-exporting-deflation-reveals-meaning-of-bernanke-s-economic
-nightmare.html

be justified by expectations of a Japan-style "muddle-through" debt-deflation scenario of drawn out stagnation and low-level deflation.[32]

Most people that aren't ultimately concerned about deflation, like the author quoted above, believe that "Helicopter" Ben Bernanke (the "Helicopter" is a reference to Milton Friedman's notion that the Fed can always just drop bags of money from helicopters if it needed to do so to combat deflation) will simply print us out of a debt-deflation scenario, like the Great Depression. Bernanke has admitted to a much larger "arsenal" (his militaristic rhetoric, not mine) at his disposal than just manipulating the Federal Funds rate. Included in the Fed "arsenal" are the purchase of more long-term U.S. debt (both public and private) and interest rate caps, like FDR had done.[33]

Ben Bernanke has been shown to be wrong again and again,[34] but even a broken clock is correct twice a day. While addressing the Japanese deflation in a 2002 talk, just 10 years ago, he explained the relationship between debt and the inability to fight deflation this way:

> Plausibly, private-sector financial problems have muted the effects of the monetary policies that have been tried in Japan, even as the heavy overhang of government debt has made Japanese policymakers more reluctant to use aggressive fiscal policies.[35] (Remarks by Governor Ben S. Bernanke before the National Economists Club, Washington D.C. 2002)

---

[32]http://seekingalpha.com/article/288974-read-bernanke-s-lips-no-depression-no-deflation

[33]http://www.federalreserve.gov/boardDocs/speeches/2002/20021121/default.htm

[34]http://www.youtube.com/watch?v=GbOWiJ94Xvg

[35]http://www.federalreserve.gov/BOARDDOCS/SPEECHES/2002/20021121/default.htm

Well, it seems that the U.S. is, in fact, suffering from the very same "heavy overhang of government debt". Bernanke's so-called remaining "arsenal" will only hasten the collapse of the American economy (and likely the global economy with it).

Money = Credit?

The Erste Group's paper 'The Austrian Approach' looks at the Misesian implication of money and credit:

> At the heart of this product lies the analysis of the development of historic money and credit statistics. It is called the 'Austrian View' because studying the theories of the Austrian School of economics (especially Ludwig von Mises' book: 'The Theory of Money and Credit'; which, by the way, will celebrate the 100th anniversary of its first publication in 2012) has inspired us to examine the relation between money/credit developments and equity prices. We have come to the conclusion that, indeed, there seems to be a connection between the two. However, it is necessary to have the right angle of vision when poring over the money and credit statistics, because otherwise they are pretty useless.

> We have to admit that it has become very difficult to determine what money and credit actually is. Money supply aggregates like M0, M1, M2, M3, sometime even M4, are being published. To complicate things further, central banks publish credit statistics as well. Finally, money and credit are just two sides of the same coin in today's monetary order. Someone's savings account (contained in the calculation of M1) is at the same time the credit financing someone else's project (contained in credit outstanding). We therefore believe that one should denote currency (apart

22

from cash in your pocket) in savings and other bank accounts as claim, not as money. We believe that M1 and M2 are good short-term leading indicators for equities. In this publication we also track the development of debt as a supplemental indicator…

The punch line is that this framework advises investors to establish long positions in equities (or overweight cyclical or financial stocks) as long as the credit supply is loose and accelerating; as soon as the credit supply becomes tight and decelerates, investors should gradually sell their positions or switch into more defensive sectors.

In this context, we would like to mention, that in December 2010 an interesting paper was published by Jordà, Schularick and Taylor, titled 'Financial Crises, Credit Booms and External Imbalances: 140 years of lessons'. They have studied the experiences of 14 developed countries over 140 years and exploited a long-duration dataset in a number of different ways (application of new statistical tools to describe the temporal and spatial patterns). Their final conclusion confirms our interest in money and credit statistics, because the overall result is that credit growth emerges as the single best predictor of financial instability.[36]

So, while money and credit are not equivalent,[37] in a fiat currency, central banking economy, where "debt is money," it certainly seems that they are near equivalents. As Hayek observed in the early 1930s:

There can be no doubt that besides the regular types of the circulating medium, such as coin, notes and bank

---

[36]http://www.zerohedge.com/news/austrian-view-approach-equity-prices
[37]http://mises.org/daily/5052

deposits, which are generally recognised to be money or currency, and the quantity of which is regulated by some central authority or can at least be imagined to be so regulated, there exist still other forms of media of exchange which occasionally or permanently do the service of money.

Now while for certain practical purposes we are accustomed to distinguish these forms of media of exchange from money proper as being mere substitutes for money, it is clear that, other things equal, any increase or decrease of these money substitutes will have exactly the same effects as an increase or decrease of the quantity of money proper, and should therefore, for the purposes of theoretical analysis, be counted as money. (F. A. Hayek, Prices and Production 1935)

A very simple way to grasp this is to imagine how loose credit can affect the prices of someone bidding in an auction. Imagine there is an antique clock that has been placed on Ebay. In an environment of easy credit, more people will be able to bid on the clock, and as they do, they drive the price upward. Once it reaches a certain threshold, perhaps dependent upon the credit available to the engaged bidders, the clock is sold to the highest bidder. When credit dries up due to bad underwriting practices (for example, subprime, Alt-A, or option ARM mortgages), the prices at auctions drop precipitously.

Look at commodity prices; they have been driven up by speculators,[38] not inflationary pressures. Simply ask yourself: is there an abundance of cash or credit, like in the stories of the Weimar Republic's hyperinflation when women brought baby carriages full of cash to exchange for a loaf of bread, or is there instead a very serious shortage of cash and credit right now? How much cash and

---

[38]http://www.spiegel.de/international/world/0,1518,559550,00.html

credit is available to you or the "average Joe" right now, more or less?

In addition to the Erste Group, Credit Suisse's Research and Analytics group has recently looked at how the debt that serves as collateral in the shadow banking system is used as money, creating "significant monetary shock".[39] Their analysis titled "When Collateral is King", while focused on shadow money (that is, securities that can easily be borrowed against), bears some similarities to mine:

- But as in any credit system, including one with conventional deposit-taking banks, the velocity of money and collateral, as well as the cost and availability of credit, tends to be pro-cyclical.
- High levels of economic activity tend to make all forms of collateral (including housing financed by conventional mortgages) more liquid, and foster over optimistic expectations about future returns, leading to asset price bubbles.
- And vice versa. When a credit bubble bursts, money-like collateral shrinks, haircuts rise, and LTV ratios fall. After major shocks such as 2008-2009 and the 2011 euro crisis the velocity of money and collateral falls steeply.
- Even so, the fragility of the financial system as it delevers leaves a deflationary undertow that can flare up quickly in response to new shocks. (Credit Suisse 2012)

Despite its apologetics for central banking, it is a good read for getting a better idea of what acts as money and credit in this age of financial engineering. Again, they are seeking a better measure of money and credit (where they include collateral) to explain the boom and subsequent bust:

---

[39]https://doc.research-and-analytics.csfb.com/docView?
language=ENG&source=emfromsendlink&format=PDF&document_id=
955237241&serialid=1U7Rr6heRpieZmFPGqcN0OvJiPMUtQgvsNOjY5
zB%2B6Y%3D

Academic research has shown a strong relationship between the severity of the shock in house prices, car sales, and (especially non-tradable) employment at the local level and the degree of household borrowing that built up during the boom. The key driver of this was the increasing value and moneyness of the housing collateral owned by formerly credit-constrained households during the boom, and the subsequent extremely sharp reversal during the recession (and recovery). (Credit Suisse 2012, 4)

Like me, they too don't see any short-term threat from hyperinflation, only the potential for more deflation. When you compare the monetary base to the total bank credit of all commercial banks, you can see that the amount of bank credit dwarfs the monetary base (see Figure 2).

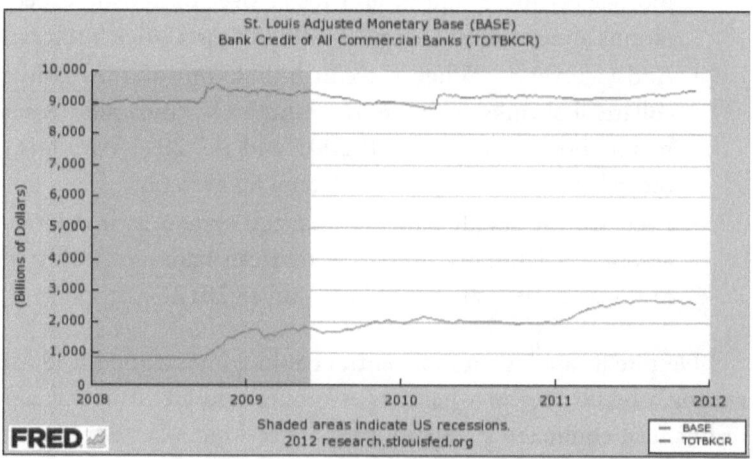

Figure 2

Bankruptcy is declared when a person or organization cannot repay the debts owed to its creditors. If you summed up *only* the largest U.S. Chapter 11 bankruptcies since 2000 (see Table 1), you'd have already vacuumed $1,591,579,372,800 (that's over $1.5 trillion) out of the economy.

Company	BK Date	Amount
MF Global	2011-10-31	$41,000,000,000
CIT Group	2009-01-11	$71,019,200,000
General Motors Corporation	2009-01-06	$82,300,000,000
Chrysler LLC	2009-04-30	$39,300,000,000
Washington Mutual	2008-09-26	$327,913,000,000
Lehman Brothers Holdings Inc.	2008-09-15	$639,063,000,800
Refco Inc.	2005-10-17	$33,333,172,000
Delphi Corporation, Inc.	2005-08-10	$22,000,000,000
Delta Air Lines, Inc.	2005-09-14	$21,801,000,000
Conseco, Inc.	2002-12-18	$61,392,000,000
UAL Corp.	2002-09-12	$25,197,000,000
Worldcom Inc.	2002-07-21	$103,914,000,000
Global Crossing Ltd.	2002-01-28	$30,185,000,000
Enron Corp.	2001-02-12	$63,392,000,000
Pacific Gas and Electric Co.	2001-06-04	$29,770,000,000
		$1,591,579,372,800

Table 1. Sources: http://www.bankruptcydata.com/ except where otherwise indicated.

And as if enough hasn't already been pulled out, there is another nearly $1 trillion in student loans in the current "education bubble"[40] that's ready to pop:

> The Federal Reserve Bank of New York recently reported that as many as 27% of all student loan borrowers are more than 30 days past due.[41]

All that money and credit being written down or charged off is deflationary. To better measure inflation/deflation, we might consider netting the monetary base, credit and shadow money, public and private defaults, and outstanding derivative liabilities.

[40]http://www.finaid.org/loans/studentloandebtclock.phtml
[41]http://www.fitchratings.com/andhttp://www.zerohedge.com/news/first-crack-270-billion-student-loans-are-least-30-days-delinquent

As if there weren't enough debt-deflation pressures, the Federal Reserve is actually going out of its way to pull additional liquidity out of the economy in the form of reverse repos.[42] This is the Fed using shadow money, or in other words, the Fed uses Treasury securities as collateral to secure short-term loans. Now, this is a short term response, likely a response to the higher gas and oil prices in the United States in the first quarter of 2012, there to help re-elect Barack Obama and perhaps to counter the fact that the debt ceiling will need to be raised again just before the November elections.[43] That indeed seems to be the case, as gas (and oil) prices are heading downward fast and are on track to hit about $3 a gallon, just in time for the November elections.[44] This is a trick of central banks around the world. In India, the RBI uses repo and reverse repo techniques to increase or decrease the liquidity in the market in a similar way. To increase liquidity, RBI buys government securities from banks under REPO; to decrease liquidity, RBI sells government securities to banks.[45, 46]

However, reverse repos weren't the main way that Bernanke deflated. As economist Jeffrey Rogers Hummel notes:

> But the most important way that the Bernanke Fed began to borrow and continues to do so is indirect and largely unrecognized: by paying interest to banks on their reserves. The Fed was originally scheduled to gain this power in 2011, but on May 13, 2008, Bernanke sent a letter to House Speaker Nancy

---

[42]See Temporary Open Market Operations for February 29, 2012. http://www.newyorkfed.org/markets/omo/dmm/temp.cfm

[43]http://thehill.com/blogs/on-the-money/budget/212313-new-analysis-brings-debt-limit-fight-closer-to-election-day

[44]http://www.freep.com/article/20120622/BUSINESS07/120622015/Gas-prices-could-hit-3-by-fall?odyssey=tab|topnews|text|FRONTPAGE

[45]http://www.svtuition.org/2011/11/repo-and-reverse-repo.html

[46]For more on collateral, reverse repos, liquidity, and deflation, please read 'Are the brokers broken' in the analysis by Matt King of CitiGroup Global Markets, Ltd. September 5th, 2008

Pelosi asking for immediate authority. Permission was therefore included in the TARP act, and the Fed implemented this new power within days.

...Not all bank reserves earn interest — only those reserves held as deposits at the Fed. A bank's vault cash earns nothing, but vault cash currently amounts to only a little more than $50 billion, less than total reserves before Bernanke launched phase two. Thus, the payment of interest on reserves was tantamount to borrowing back from depositories the full $800 billion increase in reserves and more. No wonder the impact of the base explosion on the broader monetary measures (except for M1) was so muted. Today, in fact, the growth rates of M1, M2, and MZM are declining. So phase two's seemingly massive injection of liquidity turns out to be not much of a liquidity injection at all. (Hummel, Ben Bernanke versus Milton Friedman: The Federal Reserve's Emergence as the U.S. Economy's Central Planner 2011)

The paying of interest on reserves was deflationary and netted any expansion in the money supply. Hummel also points out that, on the Federal Reserve's balance sheet, the increases in the Fed's holdings of long-term Treasuries has been almost entirely offset by the shrinking of the Fed's mortgage-backed security holdings.

Now, all this talk of deflation is really a function of the time frame we speak of. On a long time frame of, say, 40 years, we are in a disinflation right now. But between 2007 and now, we are in deflation. At any point, the Federal Reserve could hyperinflate, but it seems unlikely (unless if world governments agree to do as Myron Scholes suggests and simply erases all OTC market obligations, as described in Chapter 4). The Federal Reserve has increased its holdings of U.S. government securities to more than twice the amount it had on its books before the credit crisis (see Figure 3):[47]

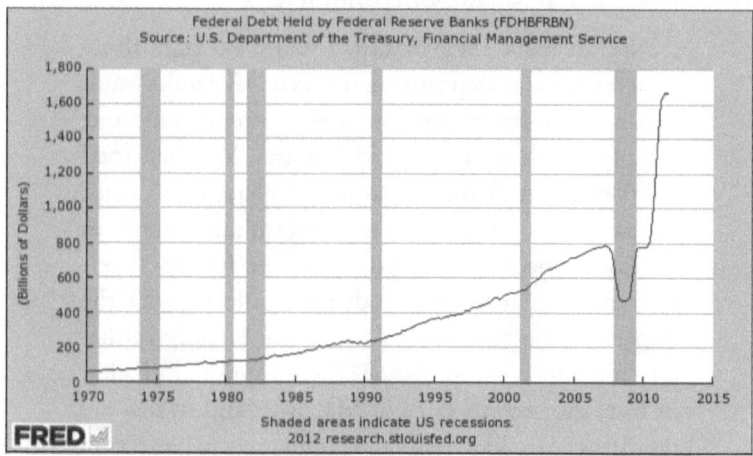

Figure 3

Assuming that the Fed is concerned with profitability (a safe assumption given the revenue it generates via seignorage, for example), it is reasonable to expect that it will behave in a self-preserving manner. If the Fed has doubled their debt holdings in Treasuries, holding up to 61% of the U.S. debt,[48] why on earth would they inflate the money supply and have the loans repaid and interest paid back in a weaker dollar? Deflation benefits creditors and inflation benefits the debtor. If indeed the Federal Reserve's interests were aligned with those of the American tax payer (aka, the surety on the national debt), then Federal Reserve would just write-off the debts owed to it by the U.S. Treasury.[49] But alas, the interests of the Federal Reserve are not aligned with the interests of the U.S. taxpayer, and as such, they will provide incentive to incur further debts without the consent of the American people.

---

[47]http://www.newyorkfed.org/markets/soma/sysopen_accholdings.html

[48]http://www.moneytrendsresearch.com/wsj-fed-buying-61-percent-of-us-debt/

[49]http://www.newyorkfed.org/markets/soma/sysopen_accholdings.html

Chapter 3

Default: Debt Repudiation And An American Jubilee

*...the most significant threat to our national security is
our debt.*
—Admiral Michael Mullen, former chairman of the
Joint Chiefs of Staff

R ECENT RESEARCH FROM the Federal Reserve Bank of New York
reveals that Americans that are over 60 years old owe nearly
$36 billion in outstanding student loans and more than 10 per-
cent of those loans are delinquent.[1] In the two decades between
1989 and 2008, 21% of all stocks listed in U.S. stock markets became bankrupt.[2] In a down economy, debts become delinquencies, delinquencies become bankruptcies, and bankruptcies vacuum credit out of the credit markets. We hear all the time in the
news of private repudiations, especially the string of people walking
away from their mortgages.[3] Now, debt forgiveness is becoming seriously considered as a part of a U.S. backed policy on mortgages.[4]
So we have an idea what happens when private debts default, but
what happens when public debts default?

In 2011, the United States not only nearly defaulted on its
debt, but it also lost its traditional AAA credit rating. The debt

---

[1]http://libertystreeteconomics.newyorkfed.org/2012/03/
grading-student-loans.html
[2]http://iopscience.iop.org/0295-5075/98/2/28005/
[3]http://www.cnbc.com/id/34207654/Should_Homeowners_Be_Able_To_
Walk_Away_From_Mortgage
[4]http://www.businessweek.com/news/2012-05-16/
mortgage-principal-reductions-weighed-for-fannie-freddie

ceiling was in the news in the last year and will come up again as we are about to have to raise it again already. Our future is clear: default. Even the guardians of the status quo must admit it:

> ...the United States would be forced into a position of defaulting on its debt. And the implications of that on our financial system, our fiscal policy and our economy would be catastrophic. — Ben S. Bernanke, the Federal Reserve chairman, addressing the National Press Club on 3 February 2011[5]

> There is no guarantee that investors would continue to re-invest in new Treasury securities. In fact, some market participants have already indicated that they would be disinclined to do so. As one of the major ratings agencies concluded in a recent report, failure to pay non-debt obligations 'would signal severe financial distress and potentially imminent debt default,' prompting the U.S. sovereign rating to be place on 'Rating Watch Negative.' — A letter from Treasury Secretary Timothy F. Geithner to Republican senators, 29 June 2011[6]

"Mr. Libertarian" Murray Rothbard provides a succinct historical example and precedent for American debt repudiation and deflation that bears sharing:

> Although largely forgotten by historians and by the public, repudiation of public debt is a solid part of the American tradition. The first wave of repudiation of state debt came during the 1840's, after the panics of 1837 and 1839. Those panics were the consequence of a massive inflationary boom fueled by the

---

[5]http://www.reuters.com/article/2011/02/03/
us-usa-fed-idUSTRE7126H620110203
[6]http://blogs.wsj.com/economics/2011/06/29/
full-text-geithner-letter-responding-to-republicans-on-debt-limit/

Whig-run Second Bank of the United States. Riding the wave of inflationary credit, numerous state governments, largely those run by the Whigs, floated an enormous amount of debt, most of which went into wasteful public works (euphemistically called "internal improvements"), and into the creation of inflationary banks. Outstanding public debt by state governments rose from $26 million to $170 million during the decade of the 1830's. Most of these securities were financed by British and Dutch investors.

During the deflationary 1840's succeeding the panics, state governments faced repayment of their debt in dollars that were now more valuable than the ones they had borrowed. Many states, now largely in Democratic hands, met the crisis by repudiating these debts, either totally or partially by scaling down the amount in "readjustments." Specifically, of the 28 American states in the 1840's, nine were in the glorious position of having no public debt, and one (Missouri's) was negligible; of the 18 remaining, nine paid the interest on their public debt without interruption, while another nine (Maryland, Pennsylvania, Indiana, Illinois, Michigan, Arkansas, Louisiana, Mississippi, and Florida) repudiated part or all of their liabilities. Of these states, four defaulted for several years in their interest payments, whereas the other five (Michigan, Mississippi, Arkansas, Louisiana, and Florida) totally and permanently repudiated their entire outstanding public debt. As in every debt repudiation, the result was to lift a great burden from the backs of the taxpayers in the defaulting and repudiating states.[7] (Rothbard, Repudiating the National Debt 1992)

---

[7]http://www.chroniclesmagazine.org/

33

How Bad is the Situation?

How bad is the debt and how bad is the Federal Reserve system? As if the reasons covered in Chapter 2 weren't enough, consider this: it was recently revealed by Bloomberg Markets[8] that, during the crisis, the Federal Reserve, after adding up all the guarantees and loans, had committed $7.77 trillion to rescuing the financial system as of March 2009. It should be clear after Chapter 2 that the interests of the Federal Reserve are not aligned with those of the American tax payer, but the money committed to "rescuing" the financial system amounts to just about half of the national debt that could've been paid off instead![9] The U.S. interest expense for fiscal year 2011 alone was $454 billion; nearly half a trillion in interest alone![10] When tax revenues and debt issuances are no longer able to pay the interest on the national debt, the U.S. will default.

Odious Debts and Unsigned Social "Contracts"

Fortunately, as Rothbard shows, America has defaulted successfully in the past, but more recently so have other countries.

> The experience of Argentina may be instructive in this respect. Argentina defaulted on its debt at the end of 2001. Its economy fell sharply in the first quarter of 2002 but had stabilized by the summer and was growing strongly by the end of the year. By the end of 2003 it had recovered its lost output.[11]

---

[8]http://www.bloomberg.com/news/2011-11-28/secret-fed-loans-undisclosed-to-congress-gave-banks-13-billion-in-income.html

[9]http://www.brillig.com/debt_clock/

[10]http://www.treasurydirect.gov/govt/reports/ir/ir_expense.htm

[11]http://seekingalpha.com/article/262724-defaulting-on-debt-is-not-the-end-of-the-world

Most recently, Iceland has repudiated their debts and even allowed their private banks to fail. Ólafur Ragnar Grímsson, the President of Iceland since 1996, explains:

> As everybody knows now, we did not pump public money into the failed banks. We treated them like private companies that went bankrupt, and we let them fail. Some people say we did it because we didn't have any other option; there is clearly something in that argument, but it does not change the fact that it turned out to be a wise move for whatever reason. Whereas in many other countries, the prevailing orthodoxy is you pump public money into banks and you make taxpayers responsible for the banks in the long run, and somehow treat the banks as if they are holier institutions in the economy than manufacturing companies, commercial companies, IT companies, or whatever. And I have never really understood the argument: why a private bank or financial fund is somehow holier for the well being and future of the economy than the industrial sector, the IT sector, the creative sector, or the manufacturing sector.
>
> So if you add all of this together and throw in the devaluation of the currency as well, it's clear that what some people have called the Icelandic model includes a number of measures and approaches that have not been adopted in other countries. On the contrary, it includes some methods in the process that go directly against what has been adopted in other countries. But the outcome is the Icelandic economy is recovering faster and more effectively than any other economy, including the British and the American that suffered from a big financial crisis in 2008.[12]

---

[12]http://www.businessinsider.com/olafur-ragnur-grimsson-iceland-2012-4

This required that Grimsson make a stand and refuse to pay Iceland's debt to the U.K., not once but twice! Doing so did not come without its diplomatic price.

> ...(*Grimson*) also blames the British for their role, specifically Gordon Brown, by whom he believes Iceland is owed an apology. Ólafur likens the situation to the Falklands war, adding it was a "great offense" that "one of the most peace-loving countries in the world, a founding member of NATO, a strong ally of Britain during the Second World War was put together with al-Qaeda and the Taliban on the official list of terrorist organizations.[13]

Iceland has even gone a step further than just repudiating its public foreign debts; it is seeking criminal charges against the administration that incurred those debts! Former Iceland Prime Minister Geir H. Haarde is being tried on criminal charges by the Icelandic Parliament.[14] What we have is an opportunity to see Iceland's response to the crisis juxtaposed with that of Greece:

> While banks and local and foreign authorities were desperately seeking economic solutions, the Icelandic people took to the streets and their persistent daily demonstrations outside parliament in Reykjavik prompted the resignation of the conservative Prime Minister Geir H. Haarde and his entire government.
>
> Citizens demanded, in addition, to convene early elections, and they succeeded. In April a coalition

---

[13]http://www.businessinsider.com/olafur-ragnar-grmsson-iceland-icesave-uk-banks-europe-2012-4#ixzz1sF292JCt

[14]http://www.nytimes.com/2012/03/06/world/europe/geir-haarde-former-iceland-leader-goes-on-trial-for-role-in-financial-crisis.html?_r=2&src=tp&smid=fb-share

government was elected, formed by the Social Democratic Alliance and the Left Green Movement, headed by a new Prime Minister, Jóhanna Sigurðardóttir.

Throughout 2009 the Icelandic economy continued to be in a precarious situation (at the end of the year the GDP had dropped by 7%) but, despite this, the Parliament proposed to repay the debt to Britain and the Netherlands with a payment of 3,500 million Euros, a sum to be paid every month by Icelandic families for 15 years at 5.5% interest.

The move sparked anger again in the Icelanders, who returned to the streets demanding that, at least, that decision was put to a referendum. Another big small victory for the street protests: in March 2010 that vote was held and an overwhelming 93% of the population refused to repay the debt, at least with those conditions.[15]

On 20 May 2012, Economist Nouriel Roubini tweeted: "Greece should follow Iceland: default and exit/devalue."[16] As much as that might be nice to wish for, in the case of Greece (and the United States, for that matter), it is unlikely to happen. It is important to note here that Iceland did eventually get bailed out to the tune of $2.1 billion by the International Monetary Fund, so it seems that they really aren't such a great role model. More importantly, Iceland's population is much smaller than Greece's (320,000 people vs. 11 million people), its unemployment was much smaller than Greece's (7.6% at the height of the Icelandic crisis is almost only a third of where Greece is today, at 21%), and Iceland's debt-to-GDP ratio was never anywhere near Greece's, 160%. Perhaps,

[15]http://www.pressenza.com/npermalink/icelandx-a-country-that-wants-to-punish-the-bankers-responsible-for-the-crisis

[16]http://nourielroubini.blogspot.com/2012/05/roubini-greece-should-follow-iceland.html

most importantly, Iceland was not part of the European monetary union and, as such, could devalue its currency in a way that Greece cannot. As shown in Chapter 2, the United States has been in the midst of a massive deleveraging and debt-deflation. Iceland's incentive instead allowed it to inflate tremendously:

> Barely, two weeks after the country's crisis erupted, its central bank slashed rates to 3.5% from a record of 15.5%.
>
> A month after that, inflation had also reached a record: 17.1%.[17]

As a result of the devaluation, Iceland's currency has now lost 50% of its purchasing power. Whether or not Greece pulls out of the European Monetary Union as a result of its crisis, Harvard University History Professor Niall Ferguson has gone on record saying:

> It's 100 percent certain that Greece will default. The only question is what euphemism will be dreamt up to cloak the fact that it's a default.[18]

I am saying that the same goes for the United States of America, too, unless the U.S. follows the path blazed most recently by Ecuador. They've adopted a tactic that could be called "truth in bonding," that is, they are operating under the assumption that long-term public debt obligations incurred through bonds should require that voters are fully informed of the obligations and that the people should be able to reject public debts that don't receive full citizen approval.

This argument is akin to the criticism raised against the idea of the "social contract." *The American Heritage® Dictionary of the English Language* defines a social contract as: "An agreement among

---

[17]http://business.blogs.cnn.com/2012/02/28/
greek-tragedy-vs-icelandic-saga/

[18]http://www.bloomberg.com/news/2011-06-15/
greece-ireland-can-t-default-like-iceland.html

the members of an organized society or between the governed and the government defining and limiting the rights and duties of each."[19] Libertarian political theorist Lysander Spooner, in his 1867 essay, "No Treason," makes the persuasive argument that a "social contract" wouldn't survive the most basic criteria for a valid legal contract because those bound by the "social contract" never actually signed any contract that explicitly granted their consent to the said "social contract". This is essentially a variation of Hume's argument against social contracts presented in "On Civil Liberty."

> My intention here is not to exclude the consent of the people from being one just foundation of government where it has place. It is surely the best and most sacred of any. I only contend that it has very seldom had place in any degree and never almost in its full extent. And that therefore some other foundation of government must also be admitted. (Hume 1742, II.XII.20)

It was in accordance with this line of reasoning that recently Ecuador officially repudiated billions of dollars of its foreign debts, although Ecuadorian President Rafael Correa seemed to employ more specifically the legal concept of an "odious debt". The concept of an odious debt maintains that public debts incurred by prior administrations that do not serve the public's best interest are not enforceable. President Rafael Correa said: "As president, I couldn't allow us to keep paying a debt that was obviously immoral and illegitimate."[20]

I would like this to be clear; I am not discussing the repudiation of private debt here. I am speaking strictly of public debts. This distinction is important because, while there are useful processes for those seeking relief from private debts, private debtors

---

[19]The American Heritage® Dictionary of the English Language, Fourth Edition (2000), Updated in 2009.

[20]http://news.bbc.co.uk/2/hi/7780984.stm

are indeed responsible for their debts. Having signed the loan documents, the debtors are legally obligated to make principle and interest payments. Such a signature or consent was never given with public debts, like the national debt. The legal precedent exists for the repudiation of public debt, and it was set by the United States:

> The United States set the first precedent of odious debt when it seized control of Cuba from Spain. Spain insisted that Cuba repay the loans made to them by Spain. The U.S. repudiated (refused to pay) that debt, arguing that the debt was imposed on Cuba by force of arms and served Spain's interest rather than Cuba's, and that the debt therefore ought not be repaid. This precedent was upheld by international law in *Great Britain v. Costa Rica* (1923) when money was put to use for illegitimate purposes with full knowledge of the lending institution; the resulting debt was annulled.[21]

An American Jubilee and the Public Policy Pivot

Land must not be sold in perpetuity, for the land belongs to me and you are only strangers and guests. You will allow a right of redemption on all your landed property.
—Lev. 25:23-28

In the Biblical Book of Leviticus, a "jubilee" event takes place every fifty years where all prisoners and slaves were set free and all debts forgiven. This old financial concept seems to be getting a lot of attention these days, even if the term "jubilee" is seldom used to describe it. In fact, in light of the political unrest in Greece and Iceland, it seems that getting rid of debt, via repudiation or

---

[21]http://www.jubileeusa.org/truth-about-debt/dont-owe-wont-pay/the-concept-of-odious-debt.html

via debt-forgiveness is a political necessity. As David Graeber, an anthropology teacher at Goldsmiths College at the University of London and author of *Debt: The First 5,000 Years,* said in a recent interview:

> Most revolutions in our history have been about debt. It is a perennial tool used by those who are powerful to make the victims of structural inequalities feel that it is somehow their fault...
>
> I think when we look back at this, we're gonna think of 2008. 1972 when the U.S. went off the gold standard was the first moment we sort of moved toward a system of virtual money where we realize that money is not a thing, it's an arrangement between people. In 2008, where it became clear that the old global financial system is something that's created politically and has to be periodically recreated, it doesn't maintain itself, like they want us to believe. I mean, that really marks a break. The question is now that we understand that money is a political construct, that they really do just print it, it is a promise that people make to each other. Well who has control over that process of making promises? Who gets to make them and to whom?[22]

Yale Economist Stephen Roach, too, is very keen on this idea of debt forgiveness to help America manage "the pain of deleveraging sooner rather than later."[23] It must be noted, however, that this notion of debt repudiation and its threat to the financial establishment is not lost on the establishment itself. A document from 1989 by the IMF's Guillermo Calvo that was not previously available for

---

[22]http://www.democracynow.org/2011/7/1/hundreds_of_thousands_of_greek_and

[23]http://video.cnbc.com/gallery/?video=3000040679

public use has recently surfaced entitled, "*Is Inflation Effective for Liquidating Short-Term Nominal Debt?*"[24] This nearly quarter century old document reveals that the IMF has been considering the impacts of repudiating national debts upon the centralized monetary system, even trying to soft sell hyperinflation as a less painful way out of crushing public debts:

> It is important to note that the inflation/devaluation bomb could be largely defused if all debt was indexed to the price level. This type of indexation, incidentally, should not be confused with floating rate nominal debt, since the latter is formally equivalent to the debt instruments that we have been discussing (and which, as shown above, could be partially liquidated through inflation). Price indexation removes by definition all incentives to inflate in order to get rid of the debt (unless, of course, the government plays tricks with the price index). From this point of view, thus, debt indexation to the price level may provide an additional, and maybe even powerful, medicine to fighting the credibility gap. It goes without saying, however, that inflation is just one of many debt-liquidation instruments. Hence, removing its tentacles does not ensure that the government will not resort to other, perhaps more socially painful, types of debt repudiation. (Calvo 1989)

So while my short time window for the immediate past and the immediate future reveal deflation on a longer time horizon, the potential for a U.S. dollar hyperinflation is real (although not palpable). According to Calvo, the outcome seems to largely pivot upon public fiscal and monetary policy:

---

[24]http://papers.ssrn.com/sol3/papers.cfm?abstract_id=884512

The main message coming out of this paper is that inflation may be an effective instrument to get rid of an unduly high level of outstanding public debt. This was shown to be the case even when the monetary authorities are unable to provoke unexpected inflation, and bonds are of instant maturity... A once-and-for-all devaluation will give rise to inflation but will not necessarily lead to an increase in the nominal interest rate. This decoupling of interest rates and inflation restores the debt-liquidation power of the latter.

The bad news of the paper is that short maturities, although a possible reaction to inflationary expectations and imperfect policy credibility (see Spaventa (1987)), are not a sure way to discourage inflation as a debt repudiation device. Therefore, the existence of a relatively large stock of nominal public debt may very well give rise to the suspicion that the government might try to use inflation to reduce the social cost of servicing the debt. Consequently, the public is likely to try to cover itself against partial repudiation by requiring an interest rate larger than under full credibility.

An easy solution to multiple expectations-led equilibria is to index debt instruments to the price level. But for that to really work, all the other mechanisms of debt repudiation must also be disabled. (Calvo 1989)

While hyperinflation is always a potential threat, as Calvo argues, it still seems unlikely. As UBS economist Paul Donovan has shown, there are strong incentives at play that will very likely keep our government from devaluing the currency.

The fundamental obstacle to governments eroding their debt through inflation is the duration of the government debt portfolio. If all outstanding debt had

43

ten years before it matured, then governments could inflate their way out of the debt burden. Inflation would ravage bond holders, and governments (with no need to roll over existing debt for a decade) could create inflation with impunity, secure in the knowledge that existing bond holders could do nothing to punish them. In the real world, of course, governments roll over their debt on a very frequent basis. As a result, governments are vulnerable to higher debt service costs if market interest rates change. If markets move to price in the consequence of higher inflation by raising nominal interest rates, then the debt service cost will rise and increase the debt. Thus a period of high inflation will tend to raise both the numerator and the denominator of the debt:GDP ratio.

As an example, the US can expect to roll over almost 45 per cent of its debt in the next 12 months and some 55 per cent over the course of the next two years. So according to UBS, if there is an inflation surge in the next 12 months, the US government would expect that to be reflected in higher borrowing costs — thus negating any 'sympathetic' inflation-impact on its national debt. There's also the issue of TIPS, or index-linked (inflation-linked) securities.

Add to that the notion that real yields tend to also rise in times of uncertain inflation — by as much as 100 to 150bp, according to UBS's analysis, as investors demand a premium for the uncertainty — which further adds to government borrowing costs.

Thus, according to UBS, the problem governments face is that high inflation is likely to generate higher nominal and higher real interest rates. This means the rate of increase in debt servicing costs will probably exceed the rate of increase in nominal GDP, as a result of the higher inflation, and voila — you have very little government benefit associated with stronger inflation, according to the bank.

The higher debt service cost becomes a problem for a government that is pursuing an inflation strategy because government debt does have to be rolled over. Unless a government is willing to pursue hyperinflation as a strategy, raising inflation will not reduce the government debt burden. Indeed, history indicates that the reverse result will be achieved.[25]

Devaluing, or hyperinflating, the currency will erode the purchasing power of the dollar and make us effectively default on the public debt. Repudiating the public debt without hyperinflating, however, would only entail the latter while avoiding the former. On 20 July 2011 — the day before the debt ceiling was raised — I interviewed economist Jeffrey Rogers Hummel about the prospects for default.[26, 27] A short while later, Hummel published the research and analysis he had discussed, and it is some of the very best on the subject. Here are some of the upsides to a default:

The most important long-run political benefit of a Treasury default would be that it would make it more difficult for the U.S. government to borrow money. In other words, a default is a balanced-budget amendment with teeth, as David D. Friedman once put it. Sadly, that characterization is not strictly correct.

---

[25]http://ftalphaville.ft.com/blog/2009/08/04/65156/
the-debt-inflation-myth-debunked-by-ubs/

[26]Along with the intrepid Joseph Fuhrig, Hummel urged me to enter into graduate school back in 1997 where I eventually earned my M.Sc. in Financial Engineering.

[27]The interview is uploaded on YouTube: http://www.youtube.com/watch?v=W7tgcBj_vzM

Many defaulting governments have proved able to go back into the loan markets soon thereafter, although often at higher interest rates. Still, a default would help to encourage both greater fiscal responsibility and lower total expenditures on the part of the U.S. government.

...In short, the inevitable default on Treasury securities will reduce taxes required in the future, and the more complete the repudiation, the greater the tax relief. How this affects the value of taxable assets, including human capital, depends on how perfectly people anticipate future tax liabilities. The degree to which they do so is a technical issue much debated by macroeconomists. (Hummel 2012)

Repudiation would impose more fiscal responsibility because creditors will be less likely to lend to the U.S. in the future, unless the U.S. proves that it can keep the national "debt-to-income" ratio more in line.

Economists regard a 100 percent debt-to-GDP ratio as a flashing warning light that a country is at risk of defaulting on its financial obligations. The nonpartisan Congressional Budget Office (CBO) has warned that the U.S. debt-to-GDP ratio could exceed that level by 2020–and swell to 190 percent by 2035. Worse, the CBO recently warned of the possibility of a "sudden credit event" triggered by foreign investors' loss of confidence in U.S. fiscal probity. In such an event, foreign investors could reduce their purchases of Treasury bonds, which would force the United States to borrow at higher interest rates.

This, in turn, would drive up the national debt even more.[28]

Currently, China holds tremendous leverage over the United States via its public debt holdings. However, the threat of U.S. repudiation has caused China, one of the biggest creditors to the U.S. enough concern that the U.S. Treasury has had to woo the People's Bank of China to continue loans us money by allowing them to bypass Wall Street and to buy U.S. debt using a method different from any other central bank in the world.[29] Will this abate the risk that China feels about repudiation and for how long? Remember, repudiation would immediately erase any leverage that the largest holders of U.S. debt, like China and the Federal Reserve, hold over the United States.

---

[28]http://www.theatlantic.com/international/archive/2012/04/
the-end-of-pax-americana-how-western-decline-became-inevitable/256388/2/
[29]http://www.reuters.com/article/2012/05/21/
us-usa-treasuries-china-idUSBRE84K11720120521

Chapter 4

Derivatives: Lessons In Bad Regulations, Bad Accounting And The Use Of Knowledge In Finance

When I ask about the origins of the crisis, economists I respect tell me it is the credit-financed growth of recent years and decades.[1]

—Peer Steinbrück

What is "Financial Engineering"?

WHEN RIDICULED THAT his poverty was proof that his philosophy was useless and impractical, Greek philosopher Thales[2] set out to prove his detractors wrong. Thales was a pre-Socratic philosopher from the ancient Greek city of Miletus who just happened to be particularly good at weather forecasting. He believed that the next fall olive harvest was going to be exceptional, so he negotiated an inexpensive deposit on every single olive press in the immediate geographical area (guaranteeing his right to exclusive use during the coming harvest season). The press owners were thrilled because they got his deposit money, even if the harvests were abysmal and there happened to be no demand for olive presses. As it turned out, his prediction was right, and the harvest was bountiful. Thales proceeded then to substantially raise the

---

[1]http://www.thedailybeast.com/newsweek/2008/12/05/it-doesn-t-exist.html

[2]Bertrand Russell said, "Western philosophy begins with Thales" (Russell 1945). Aristotle hailed Thales as the founder of the school of natural philosophy—the first person to investigate the true fundamentals of matter. The "new" discipline of financial engineering, too, traces its origins back to Thales.

price for the use of the olive presses since he now effectively held a monopoly on the process of producing olive oil in the region. Had the harvest failed, Thales would have limited his losses to only the original deposit paid. He practically invented, in Aristotle's words, "a financial device, which involves a principle of universal application." Thales, thus, invented the first recorded 'option contract' — a form of insurance. An option is a financial instrument that is also known as a derivative.

A financial derivative is called 'derivative' because its value is essentially derived from an underlying asset, such as a stock or a commodity (or in the case of Thales, olive presses). Stock options, oil futures, and interest rate swaps are all included in this family of financial instruments known as derivatives. The study and development of financial derivatives is typically the domain of 'financial engineers' or 'quants' who tend to come from math and physics Ph.D. programs, although, since the mid-00s, there has been an explosion of graduate programs in financial engineering (for example, I received my Master of Science designation in Financial Engineering in 2002 and immediately went to work in Berkeley, California, at the software and consulting firm Financial Engineering Associates). Because so many derivatives can behave as a form of insurance, a financial engineer is akin to an actuary, usually sans mortality tables and the laws governing insurance contracts (incidentally, while at Indymac Bank, I helped develop one of the first reverse mortgage servicing rights [MSR] valuation models that used actuarial tables and valued one of the largest reverse mortgage MSR portfolio at the time.)[3]

Following Thales, another significant figure in quantitative finance was a French mathematician named Louis Bachelier. His dissertation *The Theory of Speculation* (2006 (originally published in 1900)) introduced Brownian motion as a random walk model of stock price changes and demonstrated its application to option pricing. This concept did not prove very contagious until Harry

---

[3]http://www.fdic.gov/news/news/press/2009/pr09001a.pdf

Markowitz began to formulate the theory of optimal portfolio selection in the context of trade-offs between risk and return in 1952. Markowitz's Modern Portfolio Theory (MPT) (1952) marked the founding of modern quantitative finance with the idea of portfolio diversification as a risk-reducing strategy. He reformulated, in mathematical terms, the old adage 'don't put all your eggs in one basket.' Thus, Markowitz and others transformed investing from a game of stock tips and hunches to an engineering of means, variances, and 'risk aversion' indices. In fact, the term 'financial engineering' has been popular on Wall Street ever since (Mandelbrot and Hudson 2004, 65-66).

In 1965, just over a decade after Markowitz's MPT was introduced, Eugene Fama published his dissertation *The Behavior of Stock Market Prices*, which updated Bachelier's random walk hypothesis. Thus was born Fama's Efficient Market Hypothesis (EMH) (Fama 1965). According to EMH, in a perfect market, all the relevant information (public and private) is already priced into traded assets. The efficient market hypothesis is quite appealing conceptually and empirically, which perhaps accounts for its enduring popularity. *In a nutshell, efficient stock markets are generally thought of as "equilibrium" markets, in which security prices fully reflect all relevant information that is available about the 'fundamental' value of the securities.* So persuasive is the rhetoric of the efficient market hypothesis that Benjamin Graham, famous for co-authoring with David L. Dodd the treatise *Security Analysis* on fundamental analysis, was quoted as saying shortly before his death, "I am no longer an advocate of elaborate techniques of security analysis in order to find superior value opportunities...I doubt whether such extensive efforts will generate sufficiently superior selections to justify their costs...I'm on the side of the 'efficient market' school of thought" (Malkiel 1996, 191).

The Myth of Mark-to-Market: The EMH vs. Hayek

It is more than a metaphor to describe the price system as a kind of machinery, or a system of telecommunications, which enables individual producers to watch merely the movement of a few pointers, as an engineer might watch the hands of a few dials, in order to adjust their activities to changes of which they may never know more than is reflected in the price movement. (F. A. Hayek 1948)

There is a subtle but very important distinction between what Hayek says about prices in his landmark paper "The Use of Knowledge in Society" (1948) and what is claimed by the EMH. The strong form of the EMH says "all" relevant information is contained within a stock's price, whereas Hayek says, "they may never know more than is reflected in the price movement." Unlike the EMH, Hayek's assertion takes into account the asymmetrical nature of information and the limits of knowledge. This epistemological distinction is important because disregarding it has led to perhaps one of the greatest hubristic conceptual disasters in modern finance, mark-to-market accounting (MTM).[4]

MTM, or "fair value," accounting tells you that, with a mathematical model, you can estimate a true market price (the price it would sell for if you had a willing counterparty). Among quants who truly understand how markets work, MTM is more accurately referred to as "mark-to-model."

I think it is fair to say that this idea would make Hayek cringe, at the very least. Common sense tells us that secrets among actors

---

[4]The asymmetrical nature of information is why the Austrian School of Economics has largely eschewed the mathematical modeling in Keynesian economics in their analyses. See Hayek's *Contra Keynes and Cambridge: Essays, Correspondence* (1995) for more. It seems even mathematicians have come to a similar conclusion as the Austrian School in this regard (http://phys.org/news180640677.html).

exist; hence, not "all" information is available. Also, if the EMH were true, why would data companies, such as Bloomberg, constantly update their data; why is there demand for this information if it is "economically irrational?" (Dowd and Hutchinson 2010, 73)

For a short while, when I first joined Indymac, I headed the running and recording of our daily FAS133 compliance process. At the time, FAS133 was the standard by which derivative MTM or "fair" values were determined. Before this, I thought I knew what "complicated" meant. I mean, I had already done technical support for Axys and Partner — the portfolio and partnership accounting software systems developed by Advent software, I had been the Derivatives Specialist Manager at Financial Engineering Associates, and I had graduated with my M.Sc. in Financial Engineering. FAS133 has been aptly described as:

> Incomprehensible, unpredictable, unmanageable and downright frightening — FAS 133 is threatening the financial world like an alien life form.[5]

What is particularly scary is that, despite the many warnings of practitioners that adopting MTM for derivatives was a disaster waiting to happen, the FASB broadened MTM accounting with FAS157, which applied MTM accounting to all financial assets! The problem with the relationship between EMH and MTM is perhaps most succinctly summarized by Matthew Bishop, New York Bureau Chief of The Economist:

> ...the EMH motivated "mark-to-market" accounting rules, which put banks in an impossible situation when prices for their assets evaporated.[6]

---

[5]http://www.derivativesstrategy.com/magazine/archive/1999/0999fea1.asp
[6]http://www.ft.com/intl/cms/s/2/d51d6f5c-656d-11e0-b150-00144feab
49a.html#axzz1xh8SGrqf

MTM is the Esperanto of financial accounting; it created an entirely non-organic language that sought to unite the world, but instead wrought confusion and abject failure. In addition, not unlike trope in language, MTM invited moral hazard and manipulation by managers and executives who had their hefty bonuses tied to key-performance indicators (KPIs). Myopic executives could assign "fair" valuations to assets that had no true market in reality, helping them achieve their bonuses.

The Rhetoric of Financial Engineering

> In the end, a theory is accepted not because it is confirmed by conventional empirical tests, but because researchers persuade one another that the theory is correct and relevant. (Fischer Black; cited in Derman (2003))

After Fama's EMH, the next big development came in 1973. The Black-Scholes option pricing model ended the long search for a formula by assuming that the option price is independent of both the risk preferences of investors and the expected return on the underlying asset. Five years later, Cox, Ross, and Rubinstein would develop a binary model as a discrete time alternative to pricing options in place of the continuous Black-Scholes model.

This is all ultimately about understanding risk in finance. In finance, risk is usually modeled in terms of the statistical concept of a standard deviation. The standard deviation is simply the average deviation from our expectation, and it quantifies the amount of unpredictability about a particular outcome.

Most times, finance is concerned about the risk of asset prices. These asset prices are assumed to follow a stochastic process called geometric Brownian motion. A stochastic process is a sequence of random variables in time, such as the change in temperature outside right now. When you look at the zigzag line of an asset's price over time, it appears to be random, or stochastic. Geometric

Brownian motion was chosen as the metaphor for the change in an asset's price over time since the price seemed to move randomly, unpredictably.

This makes sense since the price of an asset can only be a positive number. This is why when price *changes* are modeled, which can be negative or positive, a normal distribution is used. However, when prices — not the changes in price — are modeled, a lognormal distribution is used because in a lognormal distribution only positive values have a non-zero probability of occurring. In this same way, simple Brownian motion isn't used when modeling an asset price since Brownian motion can be negative. Geometric Brownian motion makes use of the probability distribution of a random variable whose logarithm is normally distributed. Geometric Brownian motion is lognormally distributed, so it seems to make sense to use the geometric variety to model the random nature of asset prices over time.

However, the devil (as always) is in the details. Let's look at some important trope that occurs when Brownian motion is used as an analogy to describe the randomness of asset prices. Brownian motion assumes that changes are statistically independent. This means that past price changes provide no information about future price changes. If the Brownian motion has been moving down lately, there is absolutely no reason to believe that it will continue to go down (or start going up, for that matter). Unfortunately, this is not true. Fama and French found a measurable tendency for a stock doing well in one decade to do worse in the next in their 1988 study. Their 1986 study also noted price correction, a clear demonstration that prices are not independent.

Brownian motion process is also what is known as a "martingale", which means that our best guess of a value is just its current value. That is to say that, at any one time, the current price fully represents all information. The martingale assumption doesn't seem to demonstrate any anomalies, so we can let that one slide. The assumption of using a "normal" distribution is a problematic

one though. In financial markets, very large movements are observed much more frequently than would be predicted by the normal 'Gaussian' distribution baked into so many financial engineering models. Unfortunately, the models/metaphors of finance are
not often closely calibrated to reality.

Brownian motion assumes that asset returns are unpredictable
between any two points in time, and thus, they can only be described in terms of a random process that produces a probability
of distribution prices. Unfortunately, this distribution is assumed
to take the form of a normal, bell-shaped curve. It seems that just
as the changes in asset prices are not continuous, but jump about
wildly, so is it that price changes are not normally distributed.
Mathematician and the Father of Fractal Geometry Benoit Mandelbrot notes:

> So on August 4, the Dow Jones Industrial Average fell
> 3.5 percent. Three weeks later, as news from Moscow
> worsened, stocks fell again, by 4.4 percent. And then
> again, on August 31, by 6.8 percent...

> The standard theories, as taught in business schools
> around the world, would estimate the odds of that
> final, August 31, collapse at one in 20 million —
> an event that, if you traded daily for nearly 100,000
> years, you would not expect to see even once. The
> odds of getting three such declines in the same month
> were even more minute: about one in 500 billion.
> Surely August had been supremely bad luck, a freak
> accident, an 'act of God' no one could have predicted.
> In the language of statistics, it was an 'outlier' far, far,
> far from the normal expectation of stock trading.

> Or was it? The seemingly improbable happens all the
> time in financial markets. A year earlier, the Dow had
> fallen 7.7 percent in one day. (Probability: one in 50
> million) In July 2002, the index recorded three steep

falls within seven trading days. (Probability: one in four trillion) And on October 19, 1987, the worst day of trading in at least a century, the index fell 29.2 percent. The probability of that happening, based on the standard reckoning of financial theorists, was less than 105–odds so small they have no meaning. It is a number outside the scale of nature. You could span the powers of ten from the smallest subatomic particle to the breadth of the measurable universe–and still never meet such a number. (Mandelbrot and Hudson 2004)

The anomaly that Mandelbrot notes is a huge and glaring one; price changes modeled using a Gaussian 'normal' distribution will routinely overlook 'outliers.' An 'outlier' is an anomaly. It lives in the tails of distributions, tails that in financial markets should be much fatter (or exhibit "kurtosis," if you are looking to impress your statistician friends).

In stark contrast to the Gaussian distributions used by Sharpe and Markowitz, Mandelbrot suggests a much better distribution, one with much fatter tails — a Cauchy distribution.[7] I am also partial toward including the methods from Extreme Value Theory (EVT) as a standard tool in the financial risk manager's toolkit. I

---

[7]It is sometimes known also as a Lorentzian distribution. For those who speak the language of statistics, a Cauchy-Lorentz distribution has no moment-generating function. Moments in statistics simply represent the mean (the first moment), the variance (the second moment), the skewness (the third moment), and kurtosis (the fourth moment). For a Cauchy, the first moment is non-existant and the second moment is infinite, much better assumptions for modeling the unknown. A Cauchy distribution might over estimate volatility, but it's better to be overcautious in my opinion, when wagering with other people's money (or the entire global financial system). This is why it is crucial to increase the statistical power of our inductive reasoning, and by 'statistical power,' I mean specifically the probability of rejecting false negatives, as I detail in my 2009 book *Anomaly: Revolutionary Knowledge in Everyday Life*. This would likely be more of a Bayesian approach than a frequentist or Neyman-Pearson approach to statistical power.

was first made aware of this great method during my time at Financial Engineering Associates. EVT is "a specialist branch of statistics that attempts to make the best possible use of what little information we have about the extremes of the distributions in which we are interested."[8] EVT really left the blackboard when the Dutch government contracted mathematician David Van Dantzig[9] to develop a model to help prevent another event like the flood of 1953 that killed nearly 2,000 people in Holland and Zeeland. EVT was used until 2008 when it was abandoned in favor of a model based upon the Hamilton–Jacobi–Bellman[10] equation. If financial economists continue to insist upon stealing models and metaphors from physics, perhaps we can hope that they will start using models of fluid dynamics and those that employ scaling and power-laws like Mandelbrot's fractal geometry.

There are many benefits to financial engineering with regards to insuring losses, like Thales did so long ago. For example, you can hedge losses in a falling market by shorting index futures, or in a volatile market, you could set up a strategy using a 'straddle' (or similarly a 'strangle') combination of options contracts or a 'collar' (which allows an investor to limit their gains/losses in volatile times). Unfortunately, there are also great dangers presented by the current paradigms in quantitative finance. The anomalies and paradigms mentioned in this chapter have immediate and profound effects on our everyday lives. Warren Buffett, one of the richest investors in the world, has called derivatives "financial weapons of mass destruction," and rightly so. But the danger is not necessarily just the derivatives; far more dangerous are the models of quantitative finance and complicated accounting schemes (for example, schemes that claim banks don't have to book current losses

---

[8]http://www.fea.com/resources/a_evt_1.pdf

[9]I named my second child, my first son, Dantzig in honor of the incredible mathematicians that have shared that surname, including Tobias and George Dantzig.

[10]http://annualreport.cwi.nl/2009/html/realcost.html

from derivatives). In many ways, our current predicament in capital markets can be attributed to the tropes of financial engineering.

> Models are a helpful way of looking at the world. If you can get everyone to look at the world your way, then you can sell them things based on your views. This isn't dishonest. It's a reflection of the fact that the locus of financial value is vague and confusing, and any order you can plausibly impose on prices is immensely helpful to investors. Unless you can replicate perfectly and hold to expiry, a large part of value is in the mind. (Derman 2003)

VaR, Basel, and The Unintended Consequences of Bad Regulations

In the 1990s, quantitative finance would see the development of the Value-at-Risk (VaR) model as a controversial method of assessing risk that aimed to help executives answer the question: What is the minimum loss you can expect in your portfolio over a given amount of time for a given level of confidence?

In the early 2000s, when I worked at Financial Engineering Associates, one of the products that I supported and educated clients about was VaRWorks.[11] More recently, you may have heard of VaR being blamed for the $2 billion loss that JPMorgan suffered.[12] CEO Jamie Dimon tried to downplay the losses from the CIO office, but it does seem that their VaR estimate missed the volatility of the credit derivatives market, although the "exact details of the trades put on by the JPMorgan CIO have not been disclosed."[13, 14]

---

[11]www.fea.com/resources/fea_financial_varworks.pdf

[12]http://www.reuters.com/article/2012/05/11/jpmorgan-var-idUSL1E8GBKS920120511

[13]http://www.euromoney.com/Article/3024619/Inside-JPMorgans-2-billion-loss-making-CIO-division.html

[14]It is interesting to note that everyone seemed to focus on JPMorgan's $2 billion loss and not on their $5 billion gain made via the MTM "fair" value account-

The irony of JPMorgan losing $2 billion because of VaR estimates on credit derivatives is not lost on those who know the history of VaR. The ancestor of VaR was created at the behest of former JPMorgan CEO Dennis Weatherstone when he sought to find a holistic method by which to think about the risks his firm faced. Eventually, the JPMorgan Corporate Risk Management Department was spun-off to create RiskMetrics[15] to provide data for such VaR estimates.

It is crucial to understand the role of Gaussian-based VaR models used to satisfy capital-adequacy regulations in subsidizing mortgages to "subprime" borrowers (in addition to the role of the Federal Reserve keeping interest rates artificially low, of Fannie Mae, Freddie Mac, and other regulations like the Community Reinvestment Act). When you combine a bad model (VaR) with bad accounting regulations (the Basel Accords), what follows cannot be good.[16] As Kevin Dowd and Martin Hutchinson succinctly put it in their stellar book *Alchemists of Loss*:

> ...the Amended Basel Accord in the mid-1990s soon
> allowed banks to use their vaR models to set their
> market risk capital requirements. To do so, the reg-
> ulators had to specify the VaR parameters and they
> settled on a ten-day horizon period and a 99% proba-
> bility, parameters that have been ossified in the Basel
> regulations ever since. Were the regulatory capital re-
> quirements simply equal to the 99% VaR over a ten-
> day horizon, the position would (assuming the model

---

ing concept of a Debit Value Adjustment (DVA), which more than offset their loss (http://soberlook.com/2012/05/jpmorgan-made-some-5bn-on-friday-using.html).

[15]Interestingly, MSCI acquired RiskMetrics a few years after they acquired my corporate alma mater, Financial Engineering Associates.

[16]https://www.federalregister.gov/articles/2007/12/07/07-5729/risk-based-capital-standards-advanced-capital-adequacy-framework---basel-ii#p-3

were "correct") wipe out its capital in one ten-day period out of 99 such periods – that is to say, about once every three years.

A regulatory capital requirement that allows a position that blows up every three years is, to say the least, a little unconservative. To get around this problem, the regulators invented a fudge: the regulatory capital requirement would be equal to this VaR times a fudge factor, quickly dubbed the "hysteria factor." The hysteria factor was an arbitrary number, somewhere between 3 and 4, imposed on a bank by its local regulator based on their assessment of the bank's risk model.

Let's assume that the bank regulator is very conservative and imposes a hysteria factor of 4, the maximum possible. Let's assume, too, that they allow the bank to use a Gaussian model, such as the RiskMetrics one. Assuming the model is correct, the resulting capital requirement is then sufficient to meet a 4 X 2.232 = 8.928-sigma ten day loss even, an event so remote it would never happen. The regulatory capital requirements were thus reassuringly conservative.

But then again, maybe not. Recall that the Gaussian is not reliable in the tails, so let's replace it with some more tail-oriented distribution – say, the Cauchy. In that case, the probability of the capital being wiped out in any given ten-day period turns out to be 3.55%. This is a whole lot less conservative: it suggests we could expect to see the capital wiped out more than once a year.

So the length of time we would have to wait to see the regulatory capital wiped out is somewhere between a little under a year and infinity – that is to say, we have no idea. (Dowd and Hutchinson 2010, 115)

In their book, *Engineering the Financial Crisis: Systemic Risk and the Failure of Regulation*, Friedman and Kraus illustrate rather elegantly that it was these government regulations, in particular the capital-adequacy requirements in Basel I and the "Recourse Rule" in the United States which created the perverse incentives affecting both the quantity and quality of leveraged assets that U.S. banks hold. The Recourse Rule specifically encouraged American banks to "accumulate nearly a half-trillion dollars of triple-A MBS"[17] (Friedman and Kraus 2011).

Basel I and the Recourse Rule were created by the Basel Committee on Banking Supervision which itself was spawned at the behest of the Group of Ten's Bank of International Settlements (BIS). The BIS is the international organization of central bankers based out of Basel, Switzerland. Friedman summarizes:

> In 1988, financial regulators from the G-10 agreed on the Basel (I) Accords. It was an attempt to standardize the world's bank-capital regulations, and it succeeded, spreading far beyond the G-10 countries. It differentiated among the risks presented by different types of assets. For instance, a commercial bank did not have to devote any capital to its holdings of government bonds, cash, or gold — the safest assets, in the regulators' judgment. But it had to allot 4 percent capital to each mortgage that it issued, and 8 percent to commercial loans and corporate bonds.
>
> Each country implemented Basel I on its own schedule and with its own quirks. The United States implemented it in 1991, with several different capital

---

[17]MBS stands for mortgage-backed security. It is a "pool of thousands of mortgages repurchased from mortgage originators, including 'thrifts', or savings and loans; mortgage specialists, such as Countrywide; and commercial banks, such as those controlled by the huge bank holding companies (BHC): Bank of America, Wells Fargo, Citigroup, and JPMorgan Chase." (Friedman and Kraus 2011, p 13).

cushions; a 10 percent cushion was required for "well-capitalized" commercial banks, a designation that carries privileges that most banks want. Ten years later, however, came what proved in retrospect to be the pivotal event. The FDIC, the Fed, the Comptroller of the Currency, and the Office of Thrift Supervision issued an amendment to Basel I, the Recourse Rule, that extended the accord's risk differentiations to asset-backed securities (ABS): bonds backed by credit card debt, or car loans — or mortgages — required a mere 2 percent capital cushion, as long as these bonds were rated AA or AAA or were issued by a government-sponsored enterprise (GSE), such as Fannie or Freddie. Thus, where a well-capitalized commercial bank needed to devote $10 of capital to $100 worth of commercial loans or corporate bonds, or $5 to $100 worth of mortgages, it needed to spend only $2 of capital on a mortgage-backed security (MBS) worth $100. A bank interested in reducing its capital cushion — also known as "leveraging up" — would gain a 60 percent benefit from trading its mortgages for MBSs and an 80 percent benefit for trading its commercial loans and corporate securities for MBSs.[18]

Within five years of implementing this Recourse Rule, American banks had acquired nearly a quarter of the world's subprime MBS.[19] This Recourse Rule, along with the Federal Reserve's keeping interest rates artificially low, was truly a toxic combination.

By 2006, more than 90 percent of all subprime mortgages were ARMs, as were 80 percent of all Alt-

---

[18]http://www.cato.org/pubs/policy_report/v32n1/cpr32n1-1.html
[19]http://pennpress.typepad.com/pennpresslog/2012/01/the-worst-regulation-in-history-jeffrey-friedman-and-wladimir-kraus-on-the-recourse-rule.html

A mortgages, meaning mortgages to borrowers who were shy of the income, credit-score, or income-documentation standards required for a prime loan. Beginning in 2006, as the Federal Funds Rate rose, subprime borrows' inability to pay the higher reset rates triggered the deflation of the housing bubble and a widening-concern about the actual value of mortgage-backed bonds. (Friedman and Kraus 2011, 9)

The lesson of the Recourse Rule is that regulations have unintended consequences, and oftentimes, the more you try to control something, the more you actually lose control of that very thing. Friedman succinctly explains the history of capital adequacy regulation failures this way:

The theory behind deposit insurance was (and remains) that banking is inherently prone to bank runs, which had been common in 19th-century America and had swept the country at the start of the Depression.

But that theory is wrong, according to such economic historians as Kevin Dowd, George Selgin, and Kurt Schuler, who argue that bank panics were almost uniquely American events (there were none in Canada during the Depression — and Canada didn't have deposit insurance until 1967). According to these scholars, bank runs were caused by 19th-century regulations that impeded branch banking and bank "clearinghouses." Thus, deposit insurance, hence capital minima, hence the Basel rules, might all have been a mistake founded on the New Deal legislators' and regulators' ignorance of the fact that panics like the ones that had just gripped America were the unintended effects of previous regulations.[20]

Rent-Seeking in the American Mortgage Market

The United States' housing and mortgage market is somewhat complicated, so let's take a brief tour of its history. After all, in addition to the government's intervention via the Recourse Rule and the Fed's artificially low interest rates, the GSEs (Government Sponsored Enterprises), such as Fannie and Freddie, helped create the housing bubble, "having funded 45 percent of all mortgages outstanding as of the second quarter of 2008" (Barth 2010, cited in Friedman and Kraus 2011).

Just three years after the birth of the Fed and the IRS, the first GSE was created — the Farm Credit System. The government entered the home finance business in 1932 with the creation of the Federal Home Loan Banks that was closely followed by the creation of the Federal Housing Administration (FHA) with the passage of the National Housing Act of 1934. The Federal National Mortgage Association (FNMA) was created in 1938 to create a secondary market for mortgages so that those selling loans (aka "originators") could originate more loans, mostly by purchasing Federal Housing Authority (FHA) insured home loans.

As the 'Manager of Technical Oversight of Complex Instruments' in their Analytics and Valuation Group (AVG), I saw Indymac[21] become the seventh largest mortgage originator in the United States. A very large portion of Indymac's business was originating and securitizing Alt-A loans, which are more commonly known as 'liar loans' or 'no doc' loans where the borrower could qualify for a loan with little or no documentation of their income. I also saw a very serious myopic perspective, perhaps because the

---

[20]http://www.cato.org/pubs/policy_report/v32n1/cpr32n1-1.html

[21]Indymac Bank was a spin-off of Countrywide. In fact, Indymac's original name was Countrywide Mortgage Investment and was started by Countrywide CEO Angelo Mozillo.

executive management's hefty bonuses were tied to short term KPIs (key performance indicators) that lead to Indymac's having a business that relied heavily upon the origination of Alt-A "liar loans." When my well-founded concerns about the sustainability of IMB's portfolio were repeatedly ignored and marginalized, by 2006, I started to look for ways out of Indymac — and I eventually was able to transfer to Indymac's newly acquired subsidiary Financial Freedom as their "Manager of Modeling." Indymac's fate was tied to that of the GSEs, and with a pipeline full of Alt-A and Option ARM loans,[22] it came as no surprise that Indymac was the first bank to be nationalized during the recent credit crisis.

But besides being the first bank to be nationalized, why is Indymac Bank so important with regard to understanding our financial crisis? When Democratic Senator Charles Schumer from New York issued his dire warnings about Indymac's insolvency, he only hastened its demise. John M. Reich, the director of the Office of Thrift Supervision (OTS), while chastising Schumer for his public condemnation of Indymac, did eventually fire OTS western regional director Darrel W. Dochow for his role in allowing Indymac to backdate $18 million capital adjustments to make it appear as if Indymac were still well capitalized:

> On May 9, Indymac managers made this pitch to Darrell Dochow, the head of the thrift agency's western region: Let Indymac accept an $18-million deposit from its holding corporation that day but book it as if it had occurred before the end of the first quarter.
>
> In doing so, Indymac would meet an important FDIC threshold and be allowed to accept more brokered deposits and high-interest retail deposits.
>
> Dochow agreed to Indymac's proposal. The bank stayed "well capitalized" and was allowed to continue bringing in deposits for another two months.

---

[22]http://www.youtube.com/watch?v=inzm6nwbii0

In a Jan. 30 letter to Treasury Secretary Timothy F. Geithner, Reich said that Indymac's independent auditors and the FDIC also knew about the backdating plan and "raised no objections."...

"We became concerned that the bank was paying interest rates which appeared to exceed the limitations prescribed in FDIC regulations applying to banks that were less than well capitalized," Gray said.

OTS, in its role as the lead examiner, could have stopped the bank from offering those high rates.

But Indymac was allowed to bring in at least $90 million in new uninsured deposits from people like Hodgson, right before it collapsed.[23]

Darrel Dochow was also pivotal in creating the savings-and-loan scandal of the 1980s by "overriding a recommendation by federal bank examiners in San Francisco to seize Lincoln Savings, the giant savings and loan owned by Charles Keating. Lincoln became one of the biggest institutions to collapse."[24] By July 2008, Indymac Bank was taken into receivership by the FDIC.

The Indymac scandal was taken to the next level when a YouTube video titled "Indymac Boys Get Sweetheart Deal" went viral, garnishing well over 1 million views. The video charged that cronyism was at play when the FDIC was making its selection of buyers of Indymac's $13.9 billion. The assets were sold to a private equity firm headed by Goldman Sachs alum Steven T. Munchin, J. Christopher Flowers, Stephen Friedman, Robert L. Leeds, and John A. Paulson, as well as George Soros and Michael Dell.

This is where it gets interesting. As Phil Kerpen writes:

It looks like hedge fund billionaire John Paulson may have helped engineer the housing collapse that made

---

[23]http://articles.latimes.com/2009/feb/28/business/fi-Indymac28/2
[24]http://www.nytimes.com/2008/12/23/business/23thrift.html

him a fortune. Paulson, along with other notorious subprime kingpins Herb and Marion Sandler, funded a North Carolina-based outfit called the Center for Responsible Lending (CRL) to the tune of $15 million, to shake down and harass banks into making bad loans to unqualified borrowers. CRL then turned around and lobbied for legislation to undermine the burgeoning subprime market they had helped create.

Meanwhile, Paulson paid Goldman Sachs another $15 million to design collateralized-debt obligations comprised of specific subprime mortgages that he selected. This bucket of investments may have included loans that he knew were unsound and were made only because banks were strong-armed by the CRL. It also may have included loans that he knew would be undermined by the CRL's *extensive lobbying activities*. Until there is a full investigation, we won't know for sure, but it appears Paulson's $30 million – split between the CRL and Goldman Sachs – financed a scheme that netted his fund a cool $1 billion dollars.

The Securities and Exchange Commission is investigating whether Goldman acted improperly, but what about the other players in the scheme? What about the Center for Responsible Lending, which facilitated both the creation of subprime assets and their collapse, while its principal supporter made a fortune? What about the politicians who for years pumped up the subprime markets as a political pander to lower income and minority communities?

Not only is the Center for Responsible Lending escaping the spotlight of investigation, but under the Dodd legislation the CRL is poised to accomplish most of its longtime goals and achieve sweeping new powers.[25]

We will get to the role of Collateralized Debt-Obligations that Kerpen mentioned above, shortly; however, it is of interest to note here that Senator Schumer, who receives substantial campaign contributions from both George Soros and John A. Paulson, publicly attacked Indymac jointly with the Paulson-funded Center for Responsible Lending — an attack from which Paulson and Soros profited handsomely. Breitbart's Andrew Mellon writes about the conflicts of interest succinctly:

> ...John Paulson's hedge fund Paulson & Co. has been a very generous donor to Democrats. In 2007, Paulson made a $25,000 donation to the Democratic Senatorial Campaign Committee (DSCC) chaired by none other than Senator Charles Schumer (outdoing even Soros who only contributed a measly $21,750 to the DSCC that year), and also contributed $2300 each to Senate Finance Committee Chairman and Democrat Max Baucus, and Senate Appropriations Subcommittee on Financial Services Chairman and Democrat Dick Durbin. All told, during the 2007-2008 fundraising cycle, Paulson & Co. contributed $105,000 to the DSCC, $20,700 to Baucus and $19,400 to Durbin. More recently, Paulson is reported to have held a $1000-per-head fundraiser for Democratic Senate Banking Committee Chairman Chris Dodd.[26]

Dodd is the number one recipient in Congress of campaign funds from Fannie Mae and Freddie Mac and the recent subject of

---

[25]http://www.foxnews.com/opinion/2010/04/20/
phil-kerpen-john-paulson-goldman-sachs-center-responsible-lending/
[26]http://www.breitbart.com/Big-Government/2010/04/22/
Indymac-Attack--Did-Schumer--Paulson--Soros--and-the-CRL-Kill-the-Bank
-and-Profit-From-Its-Collapse

a notable scandal involving Countrywide political favors. In 2003 and 2004, Dodd benefited from "VIP" membership as a "Friend of Angelo" (FOA) when the bank outright waived three-eighths of a point on his $506,000 refinance loan on his Washington townhouse (a gift of roughly $2,000) and one-fourth of a point (another gift of approximately $700) on the $275,042 loan to refinance his Connecticut home. Additionally, since 1997, Countrywide has contributed a total of $21,000 to Dodd's political campaigns, which can be viewed through the lens of rent-seeking. *The Concise Encyclopedia of Economics* defines it this way:

> People are said to seek rents when they try to obtain benefits for themselves through the political arena. They typically do so by getting a subsidy for a good they produce or for being in a particular class of people, by getting a tariff on a good they produce, or by getting a special regulation that hampers their competitors.

Rent-seeking is unfair and patently un-American, and business people or politicians that engage in rent seeking should not be let off the hook without some sort of punishment. In the case of Dodd's participation in rent-seeking, the fallout continues:

> Give Senator Christopher Dodd credit for nerve. On Tuesday, the very day he finally admitted knowing that Countrywide Financial regarded him as a "special" customer, the Connecticut Democrat also announced that he was bringing to the Senate floor a housing bailout sure to help lenders like Countrywide.
>
> How much will Countrywide benefit from Mr. Dodd's rescue? The Senator's plan allows mortgage lenders to dump up to $300 billion of their

worst loans on to taxpayers via a new Federal Housing Administration refinancing program, provided the lenders are willing to accept 87% of current market value.[27]

This isn't going away, and it has only gotten worse more recently with the Bank of America dumping $75 trillion worth of derivatives on U.S. taxpayers with the approval of the federal government.[28] The U.S. taxpayer has become an unwitting participant, surety on the debts incurred by those that privatize profits while socialize the losses. It is a criminal endeavor; there is not a simpler way to describe rent-seeking.

Credit Default Swaps: The Keynesian Accelerant

Jeffrey Gundlach knows a thing or two about debt. His firm, DoubleLine Capital, holds the record for the fastest company to reach $10 billion in assets under management. Gundlach estimates the amount of shadow financing and derivatives outstanding at about a quadrillion dollars,[29] which also jives with the estimates of derivatives expert Paul Wilmott, mentioned in Chapter 2, who believes the derivatives market to be worth about $1.2 quadrillion dollars last year.[30] This would mean that the derivatives market is 20 times the size of the world Gross Domestic Product. As journalist Peter Cohen succinctly puts it:

> The actual cash amount of the interest rates swaps might be 1% of the $1 million debt, while that $1

---

[27]http://online.wsj.com/article/SB121383295591086669.html

[28]http://seekingalpha.com/article/301260-bank-of-america-dumps-75-trillion-in-derivatives-on-u-s-taxpayers-with-federal-approval

[29]http://www.businessinsider.com/interview-with-jeffrey-gundlach-2011-5#ixzz1vpO2SYbf

[30]http://www.dailyfinance.com/2010/06/09/risk-quadrillion-derivatives-market-gdp

million is the "notional" amount. Applying that same
1% to the $1.2 quadrillion derivatives market would
leave a cash amount of the derivatives market of $12
trillion – far smaller, but still 20% of the world economy.[31]

Raoul Pal, the man who co-managed one of the largest hedge
funds on the planet, has warned, "The problem is not Government
debt per se. The real problem is that the $70 trillion in G10 debt
is the collateral for $700 trillion in derivatives… Yes, that equates
to 1200% of Global GDP, and it rests on very, very weak foun-
dations."[32] The most recent numbers out of the BIS put the total
amount of notional Over-The-Counter (OTC) outstanding derivatives at $707,568,901,000,000.[33] Nobel-laureate and the father of
modern options pricing Myron Scholes has recently implored the
'powers that be' to "blow up or burn the OTC market, the CDSs
and swaps and structured products, and let us start over".[34] The
Comptroller of the Currency has sounded the alarm that 95.7% of
the derivatives risk is concentrated in just 5 firms.[35]

Keynes promoted an economics of deficit spending, and he and
his acolytes got what they wanted — lots and lots of debt, both
public and private. What they didn't foresee perhaps was the unintended consequences of financial innovations designed to insure
creditors against debtors' not being able to repay them — a Credit
Default Swap (CDS).

Credit default swaps were created in 1997 by the same folks
that brought us VaR, J.P. Morgan (in a unit led by Blythe Masters),

---

[31]http://www.dailyfinance.com/2010/06/09/
risk-quadrillion-derivatives-market-gdp/

[32]http://www.businessinsider.com/raoul-pal-the-end-game-2012-6#-23

[33]http://www.bis.org/publ/otc_hy1111.pdf

[34]http://www.bloomberg.com/apps/news?pid=newsarchive&sid=
aNRppMJqgURA

[35]http://www.occ.treas.gov/topics/capital-markets/financial-markets/
trading/derivatives/dq411.pdf

to hedge the risk of loan defaults. Credit derivatives allow coun-terparties to securitize credit risks that they can then buy or sell based upon what they believe their particular risk exposures may be. This allows others to bear the credit risks besides the lender and, as such, can be considered a form of insurance. However, like its cousin "life insurance" before it, it seems that credit insurance must learn the lesson of "insurable interest" the hard way.[36] While credit derivatives can act as insurance, they aren't considered insur-ance by the law, and as such, agreements were made without re-gard to insurable interest. The unfunded credit derivatives, like the CDS, include the risk that the counterparty may not be able to pay out in case of an adverse credit event. This is called counterparty risk and is akin to buying a life insurance policy with an insurance company without adequate reserves to pay your beneficiary.

The real problem with these unfunded credit derivatives is that, since the disaster and subsequent bailout of Long-Term Capital Management (and arguably well before), the true credit risk has been shifted to taxpayers. This is moral hazard writ large. The same taxpayers that never signed on to be responsible for odious debts, detailed in Chapter 3, have become an unwitting counter-party in the purchases of these derivatives, too! This strange col-lusion between credit institutions and our government has broad implications for taxpayers:

> In short, the U.S. financial system is in a delicate bal-ance. On the issuer side, a great many borrowers have linked their debt obligations to short-term in-terest rates. This is tolerated by the financial system because the debt has been swapped out through finan-cial intermediaries, so investors get to hold relatively safe instruments like bank deposits and Fannie Mae

---

[36]The Life Assurance Act of 1774, aka "The Gambling Act of 1774" made it illegal to purchase a life insurance on any other person unless the policy beneficiary had a legitimate interest in the person whose life was insured.

securities. This mountain of debt in the U.S. financial system – tied to short-term interest rates – is ultimately and perhaps somewhat inadvertently backed by the U.S. government.

On the investor side, Asian governments intent on holding their currencies down relative to the U.S. dollar have purchased a great deal of U.S. government and agency debt – effectively "buying dollars." ... A reduction of demand for U.S. short-term debt, either by foreign governments (particularly in the event that Asian governments decide to revalue their currencies) or by U.S. investors, could have very undesirable consequences.

All of which is why the U.S. is now extremely dependent on short-term interest rates remaining low indefinitely.[37]

The Federal Reserve keeps interest rates artificially low, while banks shore up their unearthly derivative liabilities with tax-payer funds, so new loans aren't being issued and bankruptcies continue to skyrocket; this new system of ENDonomics — of debt-deflation, default, and derivatives — will keep feeding upon itself until the system is dead. Take the recent rash of "bear raids" for example. These bear raids have been used to push highly leveraged firms into insolvency with the aid of CDS (further driving the current debt-deflation!). As Dowd and Hutchinson so elegantly explain:

> ...look at the economics involved. An equity short seller wishing to drive a company into bankruptcy has to take the risk that the stock will rebound, forcing it to cover its position at a loss that is theoretically unlimited; it has little leverage available, so it must put

---

[37]http://www.hussmanfunds.com/html/debtswap.htm

up an amount of money that is comparable to it potential winnings. An alternative is to buy put options; these do not have infinite potential loss, but on the other hand their premium is substantial and the time decay of option premiums is rapid, so that it has only a few months to carry out any nefarious schemes it may have.

Conversely, a CDS holder, like an option buyer, need pay only a modest annual premium, so its potential gain can be many times its investment. Moreover, CDS are typically outstanding for several years, so it can wait until market conditions are propitious before striking.

But perhaps the greatest attraction of CDS as a vehicle for bear raids is their outstanding volume. In July 2009, for example there were $1.4 billion nominal of Citigroup and $2.1 billion of J.P. Morgan Chase outstanding in the traded equity options market, while the short interest on both banks of the order of $1 billion. Yet the outstanding CDS volume was over $60 billion for each bank. For a hedge fund wishing to make an extraordinary return through promoting bankruptcy, the CDS market offers far greater buying power, lower prices and lower risk than any alternative. The choice is a no-brainer.

A related perversity is that CDS allow bond-holders the opportunity to 'game' the bankruptcy process itself. In essence, CDS holders, who if they are also bondholders can vote in the bankruptcy process, have an obvious and massive conflict of interest. In debt negotiations surrounding a potential bankruptcy, they act like spectators at a suicide, yelling 'Jump, jump' and giving their victim a helpful nudge over the edge, pushing companies into default in order to reap bonanza profits from their CDS positions.

> These sorts of problems seem to have figured prominently in the Lehmans bankruptcy, where CDS holders relentlessly shorted the stock to destroy confidence in the firm and so destroy the firm itself. They also manifested themselves in negotiations between debtholders, some of whom had nil or even negative economic exposure because of their CDS hedges, in a number of corporate bankruptcies in 2009. General Motors was the most notable of these but they also included the Canadian paper company Abitibi-Bowater and the shopping center developer General Growth Properties. Such problems also arose in the case of other institutions that got themselves into major difficulties, including AIG, Citigroup, Fannie Mae, and Freddie Mac. Short sellers got much of the blame in the media, but the reality is that CDS were to real culprit. (Dowd and Hutchinson 2010, 192-193)

When you combine bad regulations like the Basel Accords with the bad accounting of MTM and bad modeling based upon the EMH, you turn the simple insurance-like financial innovation of CDSs into a weapon of mass destruction. With the Basel Accords and the Recourse Rule, banks were incentivized to hold AAA-rated securities, since they had the lowest capital requirements, in lieu of holding non-securitized loans *that they had actually originated themselves and were much more knowledgeable about.* With a typical, non-securitized mortgage loan, prime borrowers are defined as those with an 80% LTV ratio (that is, the loan amount doesn't exceed 80% of the property's value). According to Basel I, non-securitized prime loans are assigned a 50% risk rate, while securitized AAA MBS get a risk weight of only 20%, significantly reducing the size of capital cushion banks are required to maintain by law. This gave banks a huge profit incentive to dump the loans they originated themselves in favor of securitized AAA loans.

The incentives created by Basel and the Recourse Rule weren't the only bad regulations adding TNT to the powder keg. The Community Reinvestment Act pushed lenders to loan to higher risk borrowers with products like option-ARMs or Alt-A loans (aka "no doc" or "liar" loans). *This is where the rubber meets the road;* these subprime loans (that is, loans more likely to default) began to creep into the AAA MBS tranches that were favored by Basel regulations via the credit "enhancing" nature of CDS. These subprime loans were pitched as "safe" since they had CDS protection offered by firms, such as AIG Insurance. Viola! As subprime loans go bad, banks fail since they've been incentivized to hold scores of these toxic "AAA" MBS that are backed by CDS "insurance," which do not have adequate reserves to pay their "beneficiaries." Like other forms of social engineering, financial engineering (aka quantitative finance or computational finance) is not evil in and of itself. Like a gun that can be used to rob a bank or save a life,[38] often times the intention determines whether it is good or evil. Unfortunately, as the saying goes, the road to hell is paved with good intentions.

---

[38]http://www.ncbi.nlm.nih.gov/books/NBK22885/

Chapter 5

Conclusion

IN MY 2010 book *Tea-O-Conned*, I presented a thesis that the modern Tea-Party movement would be infiltrated and effectively co-opted by the establishment Welfare-Warfare GOP. A year later the data has confirmed my thesis that the Tea Party was, in fact, no longer libertarian, but authoritarian.[1] In this book, I've presented the case for ENDonomics, the end of the United States as we know it and its relationship to debt-deflation, defaults on debts both public and private, and derivatives (of the credit variety, in particular). Given that the CBO puts the U.S.'s debt-to-income ratio at 100% (that is, the point of insolvency) around 2020,[2] that social security funds are estimated to run out in 2041,[3] Medicare is slated to last until about 2024,[4] and the looming 'Taxmagaddon,' where Americans will face nearly half a trillion dollar tax increase beginning January 1, 2013,[5] I am wagering that the collapse of the American empire will happen somewhere close to 2025, give or take five years.[6]

---

[1]http://blogs.discovermagazine.com/intersection/2011/08/17/new-data-tea-party-is-authoritarian-not-libertarian/

[2]http://www.cbo.gov/publication/21960

[3]http://phys.org/news96655116.html

[4]http://phys.org/news200247647.html

[5]http://blog.heritage.org/2012/06/15/morning-bell-how-taxmageddon-will-impact-you/

[6]Of course, there are any number of straws that could break the camel's back first, such as if the bilateral agreements that are so in vogue right now happen to kill the petrodollar. To know more, visit: http://www.chinadaily.com.cn/china/2010-11/24/

I am not alone in seeing the end come fast within view. Some states — like Wyoming — are seriously considering that the US may end and are adopting or have already adopted legislation in case the Federal government collapses.[7] When the end of the US Empire comes, we must prepare ourselves for many things — such as the end of entitlement programs like Social Security and Medicare. Regarding paying out obligations, it seems prudent that Social Security payment should take primacy in payouts over treasury securities, since social security is involuntary and treasury-securities holders assumed risk when making voluntary purchases. State assets, such as land holdings, can be liquidated, if necessary, to pay off Social Security obligations. The Bureau of Land Management is sitting on 1.5 trillion barrels of recoverable oil in Utah, Colorado, and Wyoming.[8] Selling that off to pay off the debts to social security might be a great place to start. The US State pensions are grossly underfunded, too. A recent summary compiled by The Pew Center has shown that pensioners will face a $1.4 trillion shortfall very soon.[9]

The U.S. government, as it has recently been revealed, has required banks to devise plans in case of a collapse.[10] We too must prepare. We must be exceedingly wary of those plans that the Federal government has in place in case of a collapse, called "Continuity of Operations" programs — like Rex 84 and others[11] —

content_11599087.htm, http://www.bloomberg.com/news/2011-12-25/
china-japan-to-promote-direct-trading-of-currencies-to-cut-company-costs.
html, http://www.bloomberg.com/news/2012-01-07/
iran-russia-replace-dollar-with-rial-ruble-in-trade-fars-says.html

[7]http://trib.com/news/state-and-regional/govt-and-politics/
wyoming-house-advances-doomsday-bill/article_
af6e1b2b-0ca4-553f-85e9-92c0f58c00bd.html

[8]http://cnsnews.com/news/article/gao-recoverable-oil-colorado-utah-
wyoming-about-equal-entire-world-s-proven-oil

[9]http://www.pewstates.org/uploadedFiles/PCS_Assets/2012/Pew_
Pensions_Update.pdf

[10]http://in.reuters.com/article/2012/08/10/idINL2E8J6D7920120810

[11]http://www.cbsnews.com/stories/2002/03/02/attack/main502695.shtml

and their threat to civil liberties when the collapse of the American empire is upon us. Also, know that the US Federal military also has plans to stifle dissent[12] (US Army Training and Doctrine Command 2010, iii).

Despite all this, I ultimately consider myself to be an "Apocaloptimist." Like the esteemed Johan Galtung, I believe that the collapse of the American Empire will be great for the American people. Centralized power, corruption, and bureaucrats have replaced decentralization (individual liberty being the ultimate expression of the decentralization of power), honesty, and responsibility. We are no longer rugged individualists that protect our independence; instead, we've become tribalistic whiners living in fear and in a state of dependency. The end of the United States as we know it is an unprecedented opportunity to change America's emblematic bird from the eagle to the phoenix, allowing the American Republic to be reborn stronger from the ashes of the American Empire. The works of men like Galtung and Gene Sharp[13] will become crucial to the well being of individual liberty when the American Empire disintegrates.

The End of Central Banking

Central banks are admitting they are all out of ammunition in the face of the massive, looming debt crisis. The Bank of International Settlements' economic advisor Stephen Cecchetti recently admitted, "There are very clear limits to what central banks can do."[14] The Federal Reserve has been touting its "Operation Twist"[15] re-

---

[12]http://www.tradoc.army.mil/tpubs/pams/tp525-3-1.pdf

[13]http://aeinstein.org

[14]http://www.bloomberg.com/news/2012-06-24/central-banks-face-limits-of-powers-as-debt-persists-bis-says.html

[15]Operation Twist aimed at reducing financing costs for the government by driving down long-term interest rates, since they've already driven short-term rates to nearly zero, selling short term bonds to purchase longer term bonds, using the demand to drive interest rates down.

cently, extending the "Twist" further.[16] However, a recent study by Eric T. Swanson of the Federal Reserve Bank of San Francisco has shown that the original Operation Twist was largely ineffective (done during the Kennedy administration); it only reduced rates on Treasury bonds 15 basis points (.15 percent), and one sees even less effect "as one moves from Treasury securities toward private sector credit instruments."[17]

Additionally, the IMF has recently suggested that banks will remove at least $2 trillion from their balance sheets by the end of 2013. Tim Congdon of the newly formed International Monetary Research sees further global debt-deflation, too:

> What they are doing is frightening. If banks shrink their balance sheets, it destroys money. It causes a credit crunch and intensifies the recession. This is why we are facing a global slowdown.[18]

The financial world has changed tremendously in the last 15 years, and so, while concern with the Fed is appropriate, one should also consider looking critically at the BIS, the World Bank, the IMF, Special Drawing Rights (SDRs)[19] and their proposed centralized International Monetary System to see what global central banks would like to fill the vacuum left when the American empire collapses and the dollar is no longer the world's reserve currency since it will no longer connected to the world's largest military.[20]

We mustn't be fooled into letting the IMF, the BIS, and the World Bank "save" the global economy. We must educate ourselves to their tricks and sophistry so that we may employ a form

---

[16]http://www.bloomberg.com/news/2012-06-20/ fed-expands-operation-twist-by-267-billion-through-year-end.html

[17]http://www.ericswanson.us/papers/lta.pdf

[18]http://www.telegraph.co.uk/finance/financialcrisis/9309393/ BIS-warns-global-lending-contracting-at-fastest-pace-since-2008-Lehman -crisis.html

[19]More on SDRs here: http://www.imf.org/external/np/pp/eng/2010/ 041310.pdf

[20]http://money.cnn.com/2011/02/10/markets/dollar/index.htm

of economic "mental self-defense" against their manipulations. We need truly freed markets and people smart enough to not fall for distortions (such as MTM, fiat currencies, etc.). Central bankers have been trying to buy the economics profession; we mustn't let them. As the famed economist Milton Friedman wrote to former Federal Reserve economist Robert Auerbach in 1993:

> I cannot disagree with you that having something like 500 economists is extremely unhealthy. As you say, it is not conducive to independent, objective research. You and I know there has been censorship of the material published. Equally important, the location of the economists in the Federal Reserve has had a significant influence on the kind of research they do, biasing that research toward noncontroversial technical papers on method as opposed to substantive papers on policy and results. (Auerbach 2008)

This is not all that different from the captured agencies and medical journals that we find in the pharmaceutical industry, except that the manipulations of Big Pharma "involves several companies. In the field of economics, it's just the Fed".[21] Roger Bootle recently won the Wolfson prize in economics for providing a smooth exit strategy from the Euro for countries like Greece,[22] and while this sort of thinking provides for an exit from the EU, we must endeavor forth on a research program for disengaging from central banking entirely — an academic parallel to the activist born "End the Fed" movement.

We must always heed Cicero's advice and remember to ask, "who benefits?" In the case of inflation, people with large debts (or accounts payable) would be able to easily pay off their enormous student loans and burdensome mortgages (fixed in nominal terms)

---

[21]http://www.huffingtonpost.com/2009/09/07/priceless-how-the-federal_n_278805.html

[22]http://www.capitaleconomics.com/data/pdf/wolfson-prize-submission.pdf

denominated in a hyperinflated fiat currency. The average American (who also happens to be a truly awful saver) should be clamoring for hyperinflation so that they can pay off debts incurred in the past with dollars worth less in the future. Alternatively, who would benefit from a deflation? Who would benefit by having every dollar they own become worth more? Perhaps, those who already have money and assets (bankers, the power elite, etc)? In deflation, each dollar you're owed becomes more valuable (and then again, each dollar of debt you owe becomes more burdensome).

In light of this, the good old fashioned advice is as true today as ever: pay off your debts as soon as possible. If you are an entrepreneur, it will be better to have accounts receivable than payable (assuming your clients will still be liquid enough to pay you). Decentralized money seems to be more popular these days, especially since there is a shortage of money and credit (that is, deflation):

> Francis Ayley, the founder of Life Dollars, a currency started in Bellingham, Wash., in 2004, said fear of a shortage of U.S. dollars and frustration with the growing wealth gap in the country are driving more people to his currency. Since a majority of the transactions occur online and funds are directly transferred between members, the supply of Life Dollars is unlimited, he said.

> The number of people or businesses signed up to use the currency, or members as Ayley refers to them, had remained relatively stable at 250 to 350 for years. But in the past two years, membership has doubled to more than 700. The currency's use has expanded beyond Bellingham to Seattle, too, where 75 new members have signed on in the past six months. Ayley estimates that more than $1 million worth of transactions have been made so far.[23]

---

[23]http://money.cnn.com/2012/01/17/pf/local_currency/index.htm

Conclusion

If indeed the interests of the Federal Reserve were aligned with that of the United States, then Bernanke should be seeking to write down the debt that the United States owes to the Federal Reserve. The Federal Reserve is the U.S.'s #1 creditor having lent Uncle Sam $1.65 trillion,[24] just ahead of China's $1.17 trillion.[25] We could avoid another raising of the debt ceiling by simply destroying the debt owed by the Treasury to the Federal Reserve. As we have seen, there is little chance of inflation occurring anytime soon, so there is no need to limit lending (thereby, theoretically preventing inflation) by selling off the Fed's bonds in the future to reduce the reserves of the banking system. Instead, writing off the debt would simply buy a few more years before bothering with the debt ceiling. And in the case of a Black Swan inflation event, the Fed could restrict lending (thereby, staving off inflation) by simply increasing the reserve requirements for banks! This would not only restrict lending, but also increase the solvency of the banks and reduce the risk of another "bailout." If we forgive the massive fraud of the LIBOR scandal,[26] a scandal that affects "$800 trillion-worth of financial instruments, ranging from complex interest-rate derivatives to simple mortgages,"[27] perhaps then the central banks will forgive the public and private debts currently dragging down the global economy.

> *This is the way the world ends*
> *This is the way the world ends*
> *This is the way the world ends*
> *Not with a bang but a whimper.*
> —T.S. Elliot *The Hollow Men*

---

[24]http://www.federalreserve.gov/releases/h41/current/

[25]http://www.washingtonpost.com/business/
foreign-holdings-of-us-debt-reach-record-high-china-adds-to-holdings-for-
2nd-straight-month/2012/07/17/gJQAGXalrW_story.html

[26]http://www.dailymail.co.uk/news/article-2172377/
LIBOR-scandal-rocks-US-experts-warn-biggest-consumer-fraud-history.html

[27]http://www.economist.com/node/21558281

Select Bibliography

Anderson, William L. *Wikipedia's Model Follows Hayek.* 2009-15-April. http://online.wsj.com/article/SB123976347774119699.html (accessed 2012-2-April).

Auerbach, Robert D. *Deception and Abuse at the Fed: Henry B. Gonzalez Battles Alan Greenspan's Bank.* University of Texas Press, 2008.

Bachelier, Louis. *Theory of Speculation: The Origins of Modern Finance.* Translated by Mark Davis and Alison Etheridge. Princeton University Press, 2006 (originally published in 1900).

Boyapti, Vijay. "Why Credit Deflation is More Likely Than Mass Inflation: An Overview of the Inflation versus Deflation Debate." *Libertarian Papers* 2, no. Article No 43 (2010).

Calvo, Guillermo A. "Is Inflation Effective for Liquidating Short-Term Nominal Debt?" Research Department, International Monetary Fund, 1989.

Cowen, Tyler. *Risk and Business Cycles: New and Old Austrian Perspectives.* Routledge, 1998.

Credit Suisse. "When Collateral Is King." *Credit Suisse.* 2012-15-March. https://doc.research-and-analytics.csfb.com/docView?language=ENG&source=emfromsendlink&format=PDF&document_id=955237241&serialid=1U7Rr6heRpieZmFPGqcN0OvJiPMUtQgvsNOjY5zB%2B6Y%3D (accessed 2012-29-July).

Derman, Emmanuel. *What quants don't learn at college.* 2003-1-July. http://www.risk.net/risk-magazine/feature/1497069/what-quants-don-t-learn-college (accessed 2012-19-August).

Dowd, Kevin, and Martin Hutchinson. *Alchemists of Loss: How modern finance and government intervention crashed the financial system.* John Wiley & Sons, 2010.

Fama, Eugene. "The Behavior of Stock-Market Prices." *The Journal of Business* 38, no. 1 (January 1965).

Federal Reserve Bank of Chicago. *Modern Money Mechanics: A Workbook on Bank Reserves and Deposit Expansion.* Federal Reserve Bank of Chicago, 1971.

Friedman, Jeffrey, and Wladimir Kraus. *Engineering the Financial Crisis: Systemic Risk and the Failure of Regulation.* University of Pennsylvania Press, 2011.

Hayek, F. A. "The Use of Knowledge in Society." *The American Economic Review* XXXV, no. 4 (September 1948).

Hayek, Friedrich A. *Contra Keynes and Cambridge: Essays, Correspondence.* Edited by Bruce Caldwell. Chicago: University of Chicago, 1995.

—. *Prices and Production.* New York: Augustus M. Kelly, Publishers, 1935.

Hume, David. "Of Civil Liberty." In *Essays, Moral, Political, and Literary.* Indianapolis: Liberty Fund, Inc., 1742.

Hummel, Jeffrey Rogers. "Ben Bernanke versus Milton Friedman: The Federal Reserve's Emergence as the U.S. Economy's Central Planner." *The Independent Review: A Journal of Political Economy* 15, no. 4 (2011): 507-508.

Hummel, Jeffrey Rogers. "Some Possible Consequences of a U.S. Government Default." *Econ Journal Watch* 9, no. 1 (January 2012): 24-40.

Li, Qian, Fengzhong Wang, Jianrong Wei, Yuan Liang, Jiping Huang, and H. Eugene Stanley. "Statistical Analysis of Bankrupting and Non-Bankrupting Stocks." *EPL* 98, no. 2 (April 2012).

Malkiel, Burton G. *A Random Walk Down Wall Street.* New York: W. W. Norton, 1996.

Mandelbrot, Benoit B, and Richard L Hudson. *The (Mis)Behavior of Markets: A Fractal View of Risk, Ruin, and Reward.* New York: Basic Books, 2004.

Markowitz, Harry. "Portfolio selection." *Journal of Finance* 7, no. 1 (1952): 77-91.

Remarks by Governor Ben S. Bernanke before the National Economists Club, Washington D.C. 2002-21-November. http://www.federalreserve.gov/boardDocs/speeches/2002/20021121/default.htm (accessed 2012-6-June).

Rothbard, Murray N. "Repudiating the National Debt." *Chronicles*, 1992-June: 49-52.

—. "Repudiating the National Debt." *Chronicles*, 1992-June: 49-52.

Selgin, George. "Central Banks as Sources of Financial Instability." *The Independent Review* 14, no. 4 (Spring 2010): 485-496.

Shannon, Jake. *Anomaly: Revolutionary Knowledge in Everyday Life.* CreateSpace, 2009.

—. *Tea-O-Conned: The Hijacking of Liberty in America: Exposing the Neo-conservative Infiltration and Takeover of the 21st Century Tea Party Movement.* CreateSpace Independent Publishing Platform, 2010.

Shughart II, William F. *Public Choice.* Edited by David R. Henderson. 2008. http://www.econlib.org/library/Enc/PublicChoice.html (accessed 2012-26-March).

Szasz, Thomas. *Pharmacracy: Medicine and Politics in America.* Westport: Praeger Publishers, 2001.

US Army Training and Doctrine Command. "The Army Operating Concept 2016 - 2028." *TRADOC Pamphlet 525-3-1.* 2010-19-August.

Wikipedia. *Austrian Business Cycle Theory.* 2012-30-March. http://en.wikipedia.org/wiki/Austrian_business_cycle_theory (accessed 2012-2-April).

Recommended Reading

(Mis)behavior of Markets by Benoit Mandelbrot

*Alchemists of Loss: How Modern Finance and Government Interven-
tion Crashed the Financial System* by Kevin Dowd and Martin
Hutchinson

*Engineering the Financial Crisis: Systemic Risk and the Failure of Reg-
ulation* by Jeffrey Friedman and Wladimir Kraus

The Black Swan by Nassim Taleb

X-Events by John Casti

The Fall of the US Empire – And Then What? by Johan Galtung

Risk and Business Cycles: New and Old Austrian Perspectives by Tyler
Cowen.
> Notable for explaining how mandated low interest rates pro-
> vide incentives for financial actors to take more risks.

The Debt-Deflation Theory of Great Depressions by Irving Fisher

Debt: The First 5,000 Years by David Graeber

Why Nations Fail: The Origins of Power, Prosperity, and Poverty by
Daron Acemoglu and James Robinson

Models Behaving Badly by Emmanuel Derman.
> In many ways like my 2009 book *Anomaly: Revolutionary
> Knowledge in Everyday Life*; both are written by quants (al-
> though he is leagues and bounds better than I am or ever will
> be) and both have a sections about hypnosis, the philosophy
> of science, finance, and the power of metaphors. On page
> 48 he even quotes Hayek! I am just thrilled that my book
> was published 2 years before his so that no one can ever claim
> mine was "derivative" (sorry, couldn't resist the pun)...

The Ultimate Resource by Julian Simon

91

About The Author

Jake Shannon earned his M.Sc. in Financial Engineering in 2002 and has worked professionally as a statistician and quantitative analyst in investment and mortgage banking. Having vocally predicted the recent credit crisis while the Manager of Technical Oversight for Complex Instruments at Indymac Bank, Jake Shannon also accurately warned of the current deflation we are experiencing in his 2009 book *Anomaly: Revolutionary Knowledge in Everyday Life*. In 2010, he warned about how the GOP would later go on to effectively co-opt the modern Tea Party movement in *TEA-O-CONNED: The Hijacking of Liberty in America*.

Today, Jake hosts a popular talk radio program on AM630 K-Talk and is the Chairman of the Libertarian Party of Utah. He lives with his wife and children in Salt Lake City, Utah.

For more information please see his LinkedIn page:
http://www.LinkedIn/in/JakeShannon